New Jersey: Unexpected Pleasures

NEW JERSEY: UNEXPECTED PLEASURES

Published by United Jersey Banks / Produced by New Jersey Monthly

Poem on pp. 151
Copyright © 1946 by William Carlos Williams
Used by permission of New Directions.

ISBN 0-960-4530-08
Library of Congress Catalog Card Number: 80-82041

Printed in the United States of America

First Edition

1 2 3 4 5 6 7 8 9 10

PREFACE

DO YOU REMEMBER AS A CHILD LOOKING through a screen door and focusing your eyes alternately on the mesh of the screen and then on the view beyond? In doing this, we were becoming conscious of our ability to focus selectively. In everyday life, this selectivity of focus is generally unconscious, yet it makes an enormous difference in our perceptions. We tend to focus on what is closest unless we make a conscious decision to do otherwise. This may help to explain why so many visitors to New Jersey are so often pleasantly surprised when they see our state as it truly is, and not through the mesh of a twelve-lane turnpike.

Each year, millions of people pass through New Jersey on their way to the giant metropolis of New York, to scenic New England, to the "Cradle of Liberty" in Philadelphia, and on to the nation's capital. What they see along a major span of highway tends to screen their perception of the state. The trucks, tank farms, high tension wires, warehouses, factories, and refineries create an impression that even the wide expanse of green further on cannot erase from the mind's eye. With the opening of the screen door, however, one sees that the beauties and pleasures of New Jersey abound and flourish.

Because of its unique geographical location, New Jersey's economic history has been intimately related to transportation, linking the great ports of New York and Philadelphia with each other as well as with the rest of the nation and the world. As transportation networks developed, clusters of commerce and industry developed along these arteries. But away from these arteries we find many "unexpected pleasures."

The purpose of this book is not an attempt at a precise and complete description of our state. New Jersey is far too complex, and its potpourri of activities too varied. It is the third from smallest in size, yet it is eighth in population, seventh industrially, and first in research. It has an active artistic community, expansive national parks and considerable natural beauty, with its extensive beaches and rolling mountains. To try to capture all this would be impossible in one book. Rather it is our hope, through the photographic and editorial skills provided by New Jersey Monthly magazine, to open the screen door and give the reader a good and honest feeling of what the land of New Jersey and its people are like. So often we go busily on our way and the beauty, the solitude, and the sounds pass us by.

Although one of our banks was founded in 1816, our bank holding company was established just ten short years ago. We are proud that over the years we have helped to shape the destiny of our state, and we thought the time had come to produce a book as beautiful and as varied as the state itself.

So we open the screen door and present the observations of many of us, admirers of New Jersey who have been invigorated by its industry, refreshed by its beauty, and enriched by its culture. We proudly dedicate this work to the people of New Jersey.

— E. A. Jesser, Jr.
Chairman
United Jersey Banks

— Richard L. Wines
President
United Jersey Banks

CONTENTS

INTRODUCTION 9

BRIDGES 13

IT STARTED IN NEW JERSEY .25

ENERGY 45

CARS 53

COMMUNICATIONS 65

ATLANTIC CITY 72

MEADOWLANDS 87

HEADQUARTERS 97

CRANBERRIES 111

GLASS & CHINA 121

TOWN HALLS 131

MALLS 143

PATERSON 151

EPILOGUE 163

INTRODUCTION

GRIGGSTOWN IS HARD TO FIND ON A map. This small farming town, my home, seems to be, blissfully, in the middle of nowhere. And yet, in a sense, it is right in the thick of things. Princeton and its university lie six miles to the south, New Brunswick and Rutgers six miles north. To the east, some twenty miles distant, is the Atlantic Ocean; to the west, perhaps another twenty miles, the Delaware River. On clear winter nights one can glimpse the shimmering towers of New York's World Trade Center, about forty miles away. Philadelphia's historic district lies fifty miles southwest.

Yet Griggstown seems largely the same as it must have been fifty or 100 years ago. There are more roads, of course, and more houses, but the essential rural character of the place remains intact. It is a farming community whose pulse is determined by the seasons, as it has been since the early eighteenth century. The American Revolution brought armies to the neighborhood, and George Washington stayed in a house that still stands, not far from my own. The Delaware and Raritan Canal, a nineteenth-century engineering marvel that once served as a sort of Main Street for the village, still flows with life — although canoes have replaced barges in the water, and joggers have replaced horses on the towpath. East of the canal, a hill rises rather abruptly, the top of which is supposedly the highest point on a straight line between New York and Philadelphia. Houses like mine dot the hill today, but fields of corn and potatoes still dominate the surrounding landscape. From a curve in

the road leading to my house, not far from the top of the hill, one can see the Kittatinny Mountains in the distance, and, in between, rolling fields, barns and silos, grazing cows, horses, and sheep.

If this seems an oddly specific way to introduce a rather sweeping look at New Jersey, it is even more odd for me to look back ten years and try to imagine what I would have thought had someone told me that a decade hence I would be extolling the virtues of a small town in New Jersey. I came to New Jersey because that was where I had chosen to go to school, without giving much thought to the state outside Princeton's walls, and certainly not planning to remain after four years of study. But from the beginning, there was something about the quiet beauty of the place, the stately elegance combined with a feeling of activity and excitement, that led me to put out feelers into the surrounding territory. By the time four years had passed, I felt I would never be happy anywhere else. I began to think of Princeton as home.

At first, I rode the train every day to New York, where I worked with a large publishing company, the bulk of whose employees lived in Manhattan, Connecticut, or Long Island. Some curiosity was voiced by my colleagues about my longish commute, and, more specifically, its point of origin. Their images of New Jersey led them to wonder aloud why anyone would choose to live there, and I found myself rising to the defense more than once. Yet what I defended then was Princeton, not New Jersey. It took a series of events to change my defensive to an offensive posture, and to engen-

der in me the same feeling for the entire state — that sense of belonging — which I already had for Princeton. The primary impetus behind that change was the founding of *New Jersey Monthly*.

The idea was for a magazine that would tell New Jerseyans about their state in more positive and complete terms than existing news media seemed to provide; that, through thousands of words and hundreds of pictures, would hold the "real" New Jersey out to its own residents and to the world. As I prepared for the inauguration of the magazine in late 1976, I realized that a process of personal discovery was taking place. The discovery began in Newark. For the first time, I got off the train there instead of passing on through to New York. I talked with the business leaders of the city about the magazine and how it could help them, and in the course of those talks I discovered that Newark, far from its recent image as an urban wasteland, contained the pulse and heartbeat of a massive, diverse, and powerful economy, and that there were others besides myself who saw New Jersey as the center of their universe, not as a distant planet. Later I was to discover Branch Brook Park in the spring, ablaze with cherry blossoms; Mount Prospect Avenue with its elegant apartments; the red, white, and blue cars of the city subway and the W.P.A. murals in the subway stations; the Portuguese restaurants and culture of the East Ward, and much more. But initially I simply became comfortable with Newark, began to see it as a center and as a place of opportunity. Many similar discoveries were to follow in Jersey City, Paterson, Perth Amboy, Hoboken, Bayonne, Hackensack, Camden, Atlantic City, and scores of other places around the state that had only been names on a map for me — and, I suspect, for a healthy number of other New Jerseyans as well.

At about the same time, the fabric of New Jersey's hundreds of small towns, which once seemed like so many interchangeable pieces of a puzzle, began to impress itself on me. I found old churches and gothic town halls, a thousand different volunteer groups, hundreds of elegant and unusual shops and stores, and a fierce sense of local pride. As the magazine grew, the number and variety of stories also grew, and new ideas proliferated. The possibilities were bewildering. Should we concentrate on the problems of the cities or on the prospects for business? Should we show natural wonders like the Pine Barrens and the Great Swamp or focus on the life of the Shore? Should we do Victorian houses in Cape May or brownstones in Hoboken? Above all, the central question remained, and remains: how do we go about painting a picture, a true picture, of New Jersey?

To a certain extent, the magazine has succeeded in presenting part of that total picture. But for some time we had another desire, to produce a book of photographic essays showing the real beauty and hidden pleasures of our home. Happily, our dream was shared by United Jersey Banks, whose tenth anniversary celebration led to a unique creative partnership between our organizations, and in turn, to this book.

If one thing has emerged clearly in the course of preparing what follows, it is that there is no single image or metaphor for this state, but rather a welter of images that combine to make it totally fascinating. The "real" New Jersey is neither urban nor suburban nor rural; neither paved-over nor totally green. It is all of those things, and more. This book is a portrait of that diversity. Rather than attempt to present a definitive or exhaustive picture, it offers a series of glimpses which, better than any one image or generalization, show what a remarkable place New Jersey is.

For me, there are still new discoveries to be made, new pleasures and surprises around the corner, more Griggstowns and Newarks to be found and explored. I hope that, for readers, this book is a discovery, too. For these pages are themselves a little piece of New Jersey, meant to be traversed and savored. To the extent that it leads its readers to explore and appreciate our corner of the world on their own, it will have served its purpose.

— *Christopher Leach*
Editor-In-Chief, New Jersey Monthly

Green Sergeant's covered bridge in Sergeantsville, Hunterdon County, is the sole remaining structure of its kind in New Jersey.

BRIDGES

Photographs by J. T. Miller

NEW JERSEY IS THE ONLY STATE WITH A natural, nearly continuous moat — the Hudson River to the east, the Delaware River to the west — and therefore it is a place perpetually looked down upon, from the heights of its beetling bridges, by those who enter it (the exception being those rare, burrowing drivers for whom the state becomes, gloriously, the light at the end of the tunnel). It is, for the most part, a place that one does not simply approach, but that one crosses over into, often at a price.

Benjamin Franklin described the state as "a barrel tapped at both ends," and to carry the flow at the southerly end is a bridge in his name. Built in 1926 between Philadelphia and Camden, the Benjamin Franklin Bridge was the longest suspension bridge in the world until the other end of the barrel was more cleverly paved by the lofty George Washington. Pecked out of the Palisades, this span not only bettered the Ben Franklin but doubled it, in one defiant, historic bound across the Hudson. No one before had seen a deck so impossibly thin, so sweepingly fragile, because no one before O.H. Ammann, the chief engineer on the project, had built a suspension bridge of such overwhelming weight. Its towers, too, were a novelty: rising unfinished between two states, they have never received the stone masonry covering that was intended for them. Whatever the reason for this — a pull of fashion or a lack of finances — they have their own skeletal grandeur.

South of the Palisades, connecting Bayonne to Staten Island, is another great bridge. Like the George Washington, it was conceived in the optimistic twenties and constructed during the depressed thirties; it was another Ammann masterwork; and it, too, became supreme in its class — steel arch bridges. This hanging gray hump, a pontal dromedary, is called the Bayonne Bridge, or, as nefarious a name as any bridge ever knew, the Kill Van Kull. And inspiring as it is to gaze upon, it must also be driven across; only then can one watch the constant change of piecemeal pattern, the magical unfolding of web-spun steel.

Once into New Jersey, one finds all manner of bridges, from the lowly "overpass" to the celestial "skyway." (The most famous of these, the Pulaski Skyway — which in a three-and-a-half-mile sprawl crosses two rivers, countless roadways, numerous railroad tracks, several industries, and copious marshland — has from a distance the look of a roller coaster, and, for the vertiginous, the feel.) There are lift bridges and drawbridges, Fink truss and Pratt truss bridges, yawning bay bridges and fabular foot bridges, canal bridges and turnpike bridges. There are bridges with legends: the railroad viaduct at the Delaware Water Gap, for example, under which schoolchildren press their ears to the windows of buses to hear the fatal cries of the mason, buried during construction, pleading for freedom. There are bridges that make one see double (the Delaware Memorial) and bridges that pontificate ("Trenton Makes The World Takes": this bridge-straddling industrial boast is familiar to anyone who has gazed upon the state's capital from downriver). There are bridges that may be slippery when wet. There is a covered bridge, the last survivor, roofing a bubbling creek in the vales of Hunterdon. And, again in Trenton, the home city of the renowned bridge-building Roebling family, there is a small-scale wooden version of the family's triumph: the Brooklyn Bridge. All of which leads to the conclusion that one's days in New Jersey are spent in an abridged state.
                                                    — Thomas Swick

Overleaf: The towers of the George Washington Bridge, which never received their intended stone covering, give the span a skeletal splendor.

13

At sunset the Goethals Bridge, connecting Elizabeth and Staten Island, allows motorists to experience the beauty of an industrial panorama.

Reminiscent of a Roman aqueduct, this stone bridge is located in rural Bridgeport near New Jersey's "other coast," that of the Delaware River.

Opposite: This rustic footbridge in Princeton stands at a spot where Einstein might have walked and pondered his theory of relativity.

The Princeton University crew skims over manmade Lake Carnegie, under the Washington Road Bridge.

A "pontal dromedary," the steel arch Bayonne Bridge is a model of its kind. It traverses the Kill Van Kull, linking Staten Island to Bayonne.

This railroad bridge in the rural town of Neshanic Station stands as a reminder of times when trains chugged over tranquil Neshanic Creek.

It may look like Cape Cod, but this car bridge is in Ocean County's Bay Head, a delightful New Jersey shore resort.

Inset: The "Trenton Makes The World Takes" bridge says it all, harking back to the state capital's heyday as a manufacturing center.

The Benjamin Franklin Bridge, connecting Camden and Philadelphia, was constructed in 1926. Until the George Washington Bridge was built, it held the distinction of being the world's longest suspension span.

IT STARTED IN NEW JERSEY

Photographs by Langdon Clay

ALTHOUGH NEW JERSEY'S OFFICIAL nickname, "The Garden State," remains stamped on license plates and agency seals, increasingly a tag of greater distinction suggests itself: "New Jersey: The Research State." Today, New Jersey boasts the highest per capita number of scientists and engineers in the nation. The state has more than 600 research laboratories employing over 100,000 people. Ever since Thomas Edison "invented" the first organized research and development laboratory in Menlo Park during the 1870's, R&D has been big business in New Jersey, making scientific knowledge and expertise one of the state's leading exports.

New Jerseyans have always been an inventive lot. In 1785, the metalsmith John Fitch developed the first steamboat. Another early inventor, Seth Boyden, established the first American patent leather factory, designed both locomotives and a machine for forming hats, improved Daguerre's photomaking process, and found an inexpensive process for making sheet iron. The world's first successful submarine was tested by John Holland in the waters of the Passaic River near Paterson in the 1870s.

Today, teams of scientists drawing salaries from universities and corporations have by and large replaced the colorful, enterprising tinkerers so common in the last century. But despite this bureaucratization of invention, individual genius and hard work remain the essential ingredients of scientific progress. Within the last thirty years, scientists working within New Jersey's research establishment have made such impressive discoveries as Valium, the transistor, The Telstar satellite, color television, radio astronomy, and streptomycin. (This antibiotic, which fights tuberculosis, dysentery, and whooping cough, brought Dr. Selman Waksman a Nobel Prize in 1952.) What follows are the stories of a few of the most interesting men and industries that have helped distinguish New Jersey over the years as a center of scientific curiosity and achievement.

— *Phillip Longman*

25

MASS-PRODUCED CHINA

A workman pressing out mass-produced plates, circa 1890

ALONG THE BANKS OF THE MEANDERING Raritan River and southwest toward Trenton, across New Jersey's thin waist, the soil is thick with red clay — a curse to local gardeners and farmers, but a valuable asset to the state's historic ceramic industry. Since colonial times, New Jersey's pottery makers have been preeminent in their field, setting a standard for innovation and design that remains virtually unrivaled by any other state.

The nation's first commercially manufactured porcelain was produced in Jersey City by George Dummer and associates who, in 1825, founded the famous Jersey Porcelain and Earthenware Company. Although the firm received many awards for its fine quality products, there was little market in America at the time for such luxuries and the company wallowed along for several years in near bankruptcy. Then, in 1829, David Henderson purchased Jersey Porcelain and the same year began producing America's first molded pottery with a system that made obsolete the old hand-revolved potter's wheel. For the first time, fine pottery became available at low prices, and the company flourished.

Trenton today remains a major manufacturer of ceramics, thanks in part to the vision of Thomas Maddock, who in 1873 set forth to produce the first American-made sanitary ware. At the time, there was a great prejudice against domestically produced washbowls and toilets, in favor of English brands, so Maddock took the dubious but apparently necessary step of labeling his products "Best Staffordshire earthenware made for the American market." Today, after several permutations and company takeovers, his firm lives on in Trenton as the American Radiator and Standard Sanitary Corporation — better known to anyone who has ever gazed at a gleaming sink as American Standard.

Lenox, makers of world famous fine china, is a more celebrated Trenton company. Originally formed by Walter Scott Lenox and Jonathan Coxen in 1889 as the Ceramic Art Company, the firm suffered for nearly twenty years from the haute monde's disdain for American-made china. Only after Tiffany's began ordering Lenox china for its New York counters around the turn of the century did it acquire prestige among America's wealthy families. In 1918, President Woodrow Wilson set an important precedent by replacing the White House Wedgewood with a 1,700-piece set of Lenox china. Today, Lenox china is on permanent display at the Sevres Museum in France, where only the finest ceramics are exhibited.

THE TOMATO

Robert Gibbon Johnson

IT'S NOT DIFFICULT TO IMAGINE WHAT shocked the Puritans about the tomato. "Discovered" in the early sixteenth century by gold-seeking conquistadors in Mexico, the luscious, fleshy fruit was immediately declared an aphrodisiac in England and branded sinful by Cromwell's followers. Predictably enough, their moral abhorrence of "the love apple" followed them to the New World, where subsequent generations were raised to believe that one bite of the forbidden fruit would lead to the grave. Until, that is, an eminent New Jerseyan proved them wrong and in so doing helped the Garden State prosper.

The story may be apocryphal, but in certain corners of South Jersey it refuses to yield to the correction of skeptical historians. Robert Gibbon Johnson was a prominent judge in Salem County who, along with Thomas Jefferson, was annoyed by the error and superstition of the masses who steadfastly refused to sample the innocent tomato. New Jersey and the nation needed a good cash crop to help secure economic independence from Mother England, and the nutritious, tasty tomato would serve as well as any, Johnson reasoned. One day in 1820, he decided to get his message across in the simplest, most dramatic way he knew how. Standing on the steps of the Salem County Courthouse before an amazed and apprehensive crowd, the good judge publicly consumed an entire bushel of love apples, eating one after another in rapid succession. Many expected him to be poisoned immediately, or to be himself consumed by outrageous passions. Even now, one would predict, at the least, some indigestion. But Judge Johnson remained as solid and staid as ever, and many in the crowd went home to hazard tentative nibbles of their own.

Despite Johnson's heroic example, it was not until the 1860s that Americans began to conquer their tomato squeamishness. By then the fruit had gained enough respectability to appear in Godey's Lady Book, but the recipe recommended stewing them for three hours! A turning point came in 1897, when Dr. John T. Dorrance, a young chemist working for the Campbell Soup Company, developed the world's first can of condensed tomato soup. A new era dawned.

In his effort to perfect his invention, Dorrance began an intensive quest for the perfect tomato. Breeding and crossbreeding as many as 200,000 plants, the undaunted father of tomato soup eventually contrived the now-famed "redder than red" Jersey tomato, a hardy, succulent strain combining just the right size, shape, color, texture, and taste to undo even the most fastidious Puritan. Today, New Jersey farmers annually produce 200,000 tons of tomatoes worth $20 million, making the love apple, as Judge Johnson envisioned, the state's largest cash crop.

VALIUM

Doctor Leo Sternbach

THE YEAR WAS 1954, AND THE GREAT Tranquilizer War had just broken out. Leo Sternbach, a research chemist at Hoffmann-La Roche's laboratories in Nutley, was under pressure from his bosses to invent a serviceable sedative. The competition, Wallace Laboratories, had just astounded the pharmaceutical industry by introducing Miltown, a revolutionary drug for treating patients with anxiety, and the top brass at La Roche were anxious not to be left out of the brand-new market.

Initially, the word came down to Sternbach that he should start by tampering with the Miltown chemical so as to produce a substance that would have similar effects but that would not fall under Wallace Laboratories' patents. The independent Sternbach thought such an assignment a bore. A strong believer in chemistry for chemistry's sake, he had delighted as a child in the fires he caused by mixing chemicals stolen from his father's pharmacy in Krakow, Poland. In the same spirit, Sternbach disobeyed his orders and went to work experimenting with one of his favorite substances, benzheptoxdiazine, in the hope that somehow he could devise a compound which would help his company compete with Miltown.

After two years of fruitless labor, Sternbach was yanked off the project and told to work on antibiotics, but secretly he continued with his forbidden experiments. By 1957, the errant chemist was using himself as a guinea pig, ingesting his latest compounds and keeping a journal in which he described the effects. On July 26, at 8:30 A.M., he swallowed a large dose of a substance that would later come to be called Librium and spent the rest of the day in a state of pleasant stupor.

The rest, of course, is history. Sternbach found it a bit of a problem to tell management about his secret research — at first he explained to his superiors that, while cleaning up his lab one day, he just happened to "find" an old vial containing an amazing crystalline powder — but no matter, he was on the right track. Librium not only proved a successful tranquilizer itself, but it led to further research. In 1959 Sternbach came up with a second, more effective drug. Hoffmann-La Roche's advertising people decided to name it Valium, after the Latin word *valere,* meaning "to be healthy." Today Valium is the most frequently prescribed drug in America. And it has, of course, been an extremely profitable product for Hoffmann-La Roche. So the Great Tranquilizer War was won, it seems, by a renegade.

One of the first incandescent light bulbs

Thomas Edison in his Menlo Park lab

AMERICANS, AND ESPECIALLY NEW JERSEYANS, have always taken it as axiomatic that the "Yankee ingenuity" of Thomas Edison led to the invention of the light bulb. The English, by contrast, begrudge this chauvinistic claim, insisting that we acknowledge the contribution of their own John Wilson Swan, who, as early as 1848, began experimenting with various devices which produced incandescent electric light — that is, produced light by means of continuous metallic and carbon conductors in a vacuum. There is little doubt, however, that Thomas Edison "perfected" the incandescent electric light bulb and that, because of his talents as a publicist and a capitalist, he was responsible, more than any other man, for bringing electric light into the households and factories of the world.

Ignoring the conventional wisdom of the time, which dismissed the possibilities of an incandescent light altogether, Edison in 1878 began experimenting with strips of charred paper mounted in a glass vessel from which the air had been pumped out. The result was a primitive light bulb that burned brilliantly for eight minutes and then expired. The problem, unknown to Edison, was an ineffective vacuum pump that left a small amount of air in the bulb and thus caused the filaments to burn. Nonetheless, the former newspaper boy called in reporters to announce that he had "already discovered" how to turn electricity into a cheap and practical substitute for illuminating gas — a claim that prompted one prominent member of the scientific community to charge Edison with "the most airy ignorance of the fundamental principles both of electricity and dynamics."

Stung by this criticism, Edison redoubled his experiments and eventually, with the use of an improved vacuum pump and carbonized filaments of cotton thread, succeeded in constructing a bulb that glowed for forty consecutive hours.

Trainloads of tourists soon began arriving again at the Menlo Park laboratory. Edison, however, continued searching for material to serve as a longer-lasting filament. He tested 6,000 forms of vegetable growth, including boxwood, coconut hair, cork, flax, and cotton soaked in boiling tar. As the story goes, a strip of bamboo from a fan given to him by a lady admirer at last proved the best possible substance. Edison immediately dispatched one of his men to China and Japan to collect more specimens. Other employees were sent into the Amazon jungle and to Ceylon, India, and Burma. Bales of fibers, bamboos, and grasses soon started piling up outside the laboratory. But in the end, the original Japanese bamboo from the lady's fan still proved the best. His patents secure, Edison was soon throwing all his resources into forming the nation's first electric utility company and setting up factories to manufacture the millions of light bulbs needed to replace every gas-jet in the world.

The world's first college football game, November 6, 1869

THE EXACT DATE OF THE WORLD'S FIRST FOOT-ball game is a matter of some dispute. Since the dawn of recorded history, otherwise sane men have taken peculiar pleasure in organizing themselves into large groups in order to bruise and bash one another's bodies in a more or less controlled fashion. But there can be no doubt that the world's first *intercollegiate* football game was played on November 6, 1869, in New Brunswick.

The confrontation was rooted in a longstanding rivalry between Rutgers University and Nassau Hall (which now goes by the name of Princeton). According to an ancient tradition, warring hordes of incipient Scarlet Knights would descend each year upon the tranquil Princeton campus in order to make off with a Revolutionary War-era cannon of particular significance to the Nassaumen. After years of suffering this humiliation, some clever Princetonians at last retaliated by sinking the cannon into a bed of cement (where it still sits today). Thus thwarted, Rutgers saw no alternative but to challenge the wise guys to a little friendly game of football.

A rough and ready team of twenty-five, plus fifty Princeton rooters, traveled by train to a vacant lot about 100 yards long on College Avenue in New Brunswick. Goal posts were placed twenty-five feet apart. For protection, the Rutgers players wrapped their heads with scarlet turbans. As reported the next day in the Rutgers school newspaper, "Grim looking players were silently stripping, each one surrounded by sympathizing friends, while around each of the captains was a little crowd, intent upon giving advice."

The contest was in doubt until the very end. Rutgers, deftly dribbling the ball with short controlled kicks (as was allowed by the rules of the time) scored first, only to be matched by Princeton. The violence and wild noise of the fans was too much for a Rutgers professor who happened to be passing by at the time. Appalled by the mayhem, the don shook his umbrella and shouted, "You will come to no Christian end."

At last, with the score tied 4-4, Rutgers surged ahead with a fine display of teamwork and won, 6-4. The victory did not exactly spawn a Rutgers dynasty, however. Princeton went on to win the next time the teams met, and the next time, and the next time, and the next time. Rutgers ultimately waited sixty-nine years from that first victory before beating Princeton again.

COLOR TELEVISION

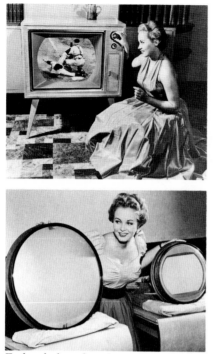

Early ads for color television

EVERY FEBRUARY 27, RESEARCHERS AT RCA'S corporate laboratories used to come under special pressure. For that date was the birthday of the now-deceased David Sarnoff, the legendary "General" who ruled over the massive electronic communications firm during its most dynamic and creative period. By tradition, RCA's scientists observed their boss's birthday by presenting him with a list of the technological innovations they had developed during the year. In 1948, however, the "General" let it be known that only one present would make the dreaded day pass pleasantly: he wanted nothing short of a fully electronic color television system with which to exploit the post-war boom in consumer spending, and R&D had better not let him down.

Actually, color television had been "invented" twenty years before, at a time when companies around the world were still struggling to develop the first marketable black and white sets. RCA's own Vladimir Zworykin had filed a patent for color television as early as 1925. By 1928, the Scottish inventor John Baird had constructed an elaborate mechanical contraption that could reproduce a moving color image by passing light through two synchronized, rotating discs into which had been drilled three sequential sets of holes in a spiral pattern, each set with its own color filter — a color television of sorts. What the world needed in 1948, Sarnoff surmised, was a fully electronic system that could be both cheaply mass-produced and made compatible with the growing number of black and white sets that were increasingly becoming a standard feature of the American living room.

The word came down to a team of RCA scientists working at the Sarnoff Research Center in Princeton that money would be no object, so long as the "General" was not disappointed on his birthday. The crash program, which was headed by Dr. Edward Herold, was given top priority and a grueling schedule: the researchers were required to prove the feasibility of electronic color television within three months and to construct an operating system within six months. The manic atmosphere made for some silly moments. During one experiment, the image of a bowl of fruit that had been transmitted from the NBC studios in New York to the laboratory in Princeton seemed out of order. "We can get the banana right," Princeton told New York, "but then the rest of the fruit is hopelessly off-color." Unknown to Princeton, a prankster in New York had painted the banana blue.

Despite the horseplay, the team succeeded in inventing the shadow mask picture tube, the missing link in the development of color television, in time for the "General's" birthday. With this stroke, RCA stole the lead from CBS, Philco, and other companies engaged in the competitive struggle for a marketable color television system. And before long, the entire industry had adopted the new technology.

BALL BEARINGS

A roller bearing factory in Trenton

IMAGINE A WORLD WITHOUT BALL BEARINGS, a frictional world in which automobile engines jam up and melt, baby carriage wheels smoke, and propellor shafts grind away in slow motion. Since the beginning of the twentieth century, ball bearing plants have become one of the most strategic targets in any war, for without a good supply of these tiny, shiny pellets, any technologically advanced nation would literally go up in smoke.

Most likely it was the Italian Renaissance sculptor and goldsmith, Benvenuto Cellini (1500-1571), who first saw the potential of a circle of freely revolving balls to reduce the friction between two rotating bodies. Cellini boasts in his autobiography that in 1543, "having finished the beautiful statue of Jupiter, I placed it upon a wooden base, and within it I fixed four little globes of wood which were more than half hidden in their sockets and so admirably contrived that a little child could, with the utmost ease, move the statue backwards and forwards and turn it round."

Several centuries passed before ball bearings found other applications. During the last quarter of the eighteenth century they were used to increase the efficiency of windmills. In 1794, Philip Vaughan, an ironmaster of Carmarthen, Wales, patented the first radial ball bearings and used them in the axle-bearing of a carriage. As the world became faster and more mechanically sophisticated in the nineteenth century, ball bearings became increasingly important: every new invention that turned, rotated, spun, or swung, from merry-go-rounds and gun turrets to armchairs and bicycle wheels, relied on the perfection of the tiny ball bearing.

In New Jersey, Mathius Pfatischer, the chief engineer of the Electro Dynamic Company of Bayonne (now a subsidiary of General Dynamics), was the first to install ball bearings in an electric motor. Pfatischer's rugged, direct-current Interpol motor, patented in 1904, became so popular for its ability to operate at a wide range of speeds without sparking that it was soon widely pirated. The little motor and the ball bearings inside it made unnecessary the elaborate and trouble-prone system of belts and wheels that were once commonly used to power small factory machines. Innovation is not without its controversies. During 1907, in one of the most hotly fought legal battles in electrical history, Electro-Dynamics brought an infringement-of-patents suit against Westinghouse and lost on the grounds that Pfatischer's invention was not original. But this shouldn't detract from his achievement. The very fact that the suit was brought and so bitterly contested testifies to the importance of Pfatischer's contribution.

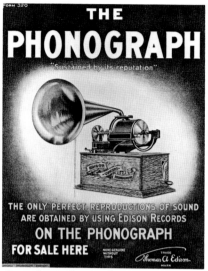

*An early window card
promoting Edison's phonograph*

*Young Thomas Edison
with his new "talking machine"*

THEY CALLED HIM "THE NEW JERSEY COLUMbus" and "the wizard of Menlo Park." His rustic neighbors in Metuchen told tales of machines that could overhear farmers talking — or even cows munching grass — a mile away. When, at age 30, Thomas A. Edison invented the phonograph, throngs of tourists from all over the country crowded on special excursion trains bound for "the village of science" that had grown up around the famous inventor in the New Jersey countryside.

Sometime during the late summer or early fall of 1877, Edison dashed off a sketch of the world's first phonograph and handed it to one of his workmen with the note, "Kruesi, Make this — Edison." Kruesi was charged to follow the specifications exactly and to spend no more than $18. By the time the poor workman was finished with his assignment, he still hadn't figured out what it was for. In explanation, his boss informed him laconically: "The machine must talk." Kruesi scratched his head in disbelief. Other workers bet cigars with "the Old Man," as Edison was already called, that the contraption would not work. The improbable device was made of brass and iron, with a three-and-a-half-inch cylinder on a foot-long shaft; it had a hand crank to turn it; two diaphragms, each with a stylus, were mounted in adjustable tubes at opposite sides of the cylinder, around which Edison wrapped a sheet of tin foil to record the movements of the diaphragm.

When the model was ready, the entire laboratory staff gathered around the inventor as he prepared the machine for its first test. Turning the cylinder by means of the crank, Edison shouted into the mouthpiece:

> *Mary had a little lamb,*
> *Its fleece was white as snow.*
> *And everywhere that Mary went,*
> *The lamb was sure to go.*

Amid the joking and laughing of his men, Edison calmly turned back the cylinder, adjusted the reproducing diaphragm, and once more rotated the cylinder. He expected to hear only an encouraging fragment of sound or to obtain a few recognizable squeaks at best, something to show at least that he was on the right track. But, instead, to his astonishment, he heard the distinct sound of his own voice: the words of the nursery rhyme were reproduced, as he later recalled, "almost perfectly." Kruesi turned pale and made some pious exclamation in German. The other workers were dumbfounded. Within a year, their boss would be famous all over the world, lionized at the White House and heralded in the papers as "one of the wonders of the world."

CELLULOID

John Wesley Hyatt

Hyatt's lathe for turning billiard balls

THE MOST PLEASING STORIES BEHIND GREAT inventions are those that involve ingenious amateurs who, while looking for something trivial, stumble upon something monumental — and have the good sense to realize it. Such is the case with celluloid, the versatile substance that revolutionized photography and cinema, not to mention men's shirt collars. Central to this story is John Wesley Hyatt, a young tinkerer from upstate New York who made his mark, as the father of the plastic industry, in Newark.

During the mid-nineteenth century, ivory was becoming increasingly scarce and expensive. A company in New York, Phelan & Collander, attracted the young Hyatt's attention by offering a prize of $10,000 to the first person who could devise or discover a cheap substitute for the ivory then used to make billiard balls. Working nights and Sundays, Hyatt, who was untutored in chemistry and unaware of the work of other inventors in the field, experimented with an extremely dangerous mixture of chemicals, including paper flack, shellac, and collodion, in an attempt to win the prize. Eventually he succeeded, and his formula is still commonly used in the manufacture of billiard balls. (Today, however, pool players don't have to contend with the major drawback of Hyatt's original formula: flammability. The chief constituent of Hyatt's new substance was cellulose nitrate, or nitrocellulose, a volatile chemical that caused the new billiard balls to burst into flame when struck even by a cigar ash. In fact, when two balls collided violently enough, a mild explosion would result: Hyatt once received a letter from a Colorado saloon keeper complaining that every time a hard-hit ball exploded, his customers would leap for their guns.)

In the process of developing the modern billiard ball, though, Hyatt was led to a more important contribution. During his experiments, he was drawn to the dry "artificial skin" that formed on the surface of the balls when drying. Continuing his research, Hyatt and his brother Isaiah eventually discovered the crucial fact upon which the invention of celluloid is based: that a mixture of nitrocellulose, camphor, and a small amount of alcohol can be made soft enough by heat to mold but becomes hard again under atmospheric conditions. Within a few years, he perfected the complicated technique and was able, with the backing of some New York investors, to construct the world's first celluloid factory in Newark.

ENERGY

Photographs by Allan Weitz

THERE'S A LITTLE PEAT IN THE PINE Barrens, the oil companies are drilling exploratory wells off the coast of Atlantic City, and pilot projects are under way for the burning of municipal garbage. That's the sum total of New Jersey's home-grown energy resources, and it doesn't add up to much when you consider that the state uses more than 600,000 barrels of petroleum each day.

But if New Jersey comes up short in this particular energy equation, it makes up for it with brain power. For this small, densely populated state of seven million people is home to one of the greatest concentrations of energy expertise in the country.

Not only is the major research arm of the Exxon Corporation located in Linden and Florham Park, but Mobil has its Research and Development Corporation in Paulsboro and Princeton. Companies like Hydrocarbon Research Incorporated in Lawrence Township are contracting with industry and government for specialized energy projects, and myriad specialists are working at universities throughout the state.

"When you come to the liquefaction of coal into oil, for example, three-quarters of the technical expertise in the nation resides right here in New Jersey," says one state energy expert. "We have tremendous scientific and technical talent within our state."

One reason is that New Jersey has one of the densest concentrations of petroleum refining capacity in the Northeast. There is Exxon's Bayway facility in Linden, capable of

refining 290,000 barrels of crude oil each day; Chevron's 168,000-barrel refinery in Perth Amboy; the 98,000-barrel Mobil refinery in Paulsboro; and the 90,000-barrel Texaco facility in Westville. Located along major highways, these massive refineries have helped to make New Jersey's industrial landscape famous. With sprawling tank farms, giant processing towers, and eternal flames that burn off otherwise uncapturable gas fumes, they epitomize industrial America. Yet the real strength of the petroleum industry in New Jersey is not in the refineries. It is in the laboratories.

The giant Exxon Corporation started in 1882 as Standard Oil of New Jersey. In 1909, the company opened its Bayway Refinery, and in 1919 a special research division was established at the refinery. By 1948, the research division had grown so large that it needed its own seventy-acre site in Linden. Today, the Exxon Research and Engineering Company, headquartered in Florham Park, has 3,500 employees at five sites across the United States and in England.

It was in the forties that Exxon scientists in New Jersey developed the fluid catalytic cracking process that increased the refineries' capacity to produce high-octane fuels. And in the 1960s, it was Mobil research scientists at Paulsboro who developed a catalyst that increased the yield from a barrel of crude oil by one-third.

Today, the laboratories are still looking for ways to stretch a barrel of crude, but they are also exploring more exotic fields like synthetic fuels, coal liquefaction, and solar energy. Hydrocarbon Research, for one, is studying the use of "junk" fuel sources such as tar sands, shale, and refinery waste. And Mobil has learned how to produce gasoline from coal-derived

Opposite: Exxon's Bayway Refinery in Linden takes on an ethereal brilliance at night. 290,000 barrels of oil are processed each day.

methanol. Public Service Electric and Gas Company (PSE&G) is experimenting with fuel cell power plants, and Engelhard Industries is working with catalytic converters.

The experiments, however, aren't limited to the research labs. The City of Trenton, for example, has government funding for an integrated community energy system in which "waste" heat from an electrical power plant will be used to heat and cool state office buildings. Another project includes sophisticated energy-monitoring of the high-rise Newark office building that serves as headquarters for PSE&G. The New Jersey Energy Research Institute is largely responsible for these efforts. A consortium of private businesses, government, universities, and utilities, NJERI believes that New Jersey's population density and high energy use make the state a perfect energy laboratory.

Yet it is the work being done at the Princeton University Plasma Physics Laboratory that is likely to have the biggest impact on our energy future. Here physicists have been working for nearly thirty years to develop a practical form of fusion energy. For many scientists, fusion represents the way of the future: it promises boundless nuclear energy from the same process that fuels the sun, along with far fewer risks than current fission techniques entail. To the scientists at Princeton, the question is not *whether* they will be able to harness fusion power, but when.

The Princeton site, the largest of four magnetic fusion research facilities in the country, will soon house the first reactor capable of producing significant amounts of fusion energy. When the $284-million project is completed in 1981, scientists hope to reach the break-even point, the point at which they can create as much "new" energy as they use up in the process of creation.

That makes Princeton an important place in the international scientific community. But the quiet branch campus located along Route 1 has attracted little attention from non-scientists. No one expects fusion energy to make a significant contribution until the twenty-first century, so the scientists work on their giant test reactors in relative anonymity.

Yet there is a sense of history-in-the-making that hovers over the spacious green lawns and secluded laboratory buildings where hydrogen is fused into helium at temperatures of 80 million degrees and up. Perhaps it is the knowledge that the site once housed top-secret research on the hydrogen bomb. More likely, it is the scientists' belief that the day of fusion power is fast approaching.

As one staff member proudly says: "When people look back on the twentieth century eons from now, they'll remember it for just two things — man's first venture into space and the harnessing of fusion energy."

— *Lynn Asinof*

There is beauty in the most functional of structures, as shown in this photograph of PSE&G storage tanks along the Turnpike.

Overleaf: The Hess refinery in Port Reading has helped make New Jersey one of the top petroleum processing states in America, and possesses a kind of utilitarian magnificence.

Commercial energy is provided by the Salem Nuclear Generating Plant in Lower Alloways Creek, Salem County. Salem I began functioning in early 1977. Salem II will eventually provide electricity for 500,000 people.

Top: Workmen putting finishing touches on the Salem II containment vessel.

Above: These eerie green pipes are part of the circulation system of Salem II.

Brightly painted stock cars and the smell of burning rubber add to the excitement at Englishtown's Raceway Park, where a national meet draws more than 40,000 hot rod fans.

CARS

Photographs by J. T. Miller

ROCK AND ROLL SINGER BRUCE SPRING-steen is home-grown New Jersey, yet when "The Boss" writes about the Garden State he doesn't even mention tomatoes: "Man, there's an opera out on the Turnpike." Springsteen's New Jersey is the world of "the Pike," Route 9, Dodges, and the local police — the "Cherry Tops." For many others, too, life in New Jersey is life on the road, the culture of highways and cars.

No small wonder: New Jersey has the highest traffic density of any state on the East Coast, and although parts of California have higher traffic densities than New Jersey — Los Angeles County itself has more cars than all of New Jersey — its density statewide is lower than ours. Thousands of cars are unloaded daily from ships at Port Newark for sale throughout the East. The importers like to keep their figures secret, but Port Authority and state trade officials estimate that upwards of 300,000 cars pass through Port Newark yearly. "It looks like the Indianapolis 500 out there," says one Port Authority official, marveling at the stream of cars flowing from the ships.

Fifteen of the top foreign car companies maintain their American headquarters in New Jersey: Toyota, Datsun, Honda, Subaru, Fiat, BMW, Mercedes-Benz, Volkswagen, Volvo, Alfa-Romeo, Peugeot, Mazda, Jaguar/Rover-Triumph, Renault, and Rolls-Royce. (The only prominent name not on the list is Saab: it's in Orange, Connecticut.) In fact, there is so much imported car activity in New Jersey that the federal government has opened an auto testing labo-ratory in Newark on Routes 1 and 9 so that the imports don't have to be driven to Washington, D.C., or Detroit to see if they meet federal standards for safety and emissions.

New Jersey is also a producer of cars. There are four auto plants in the state, churning out everything from subcompacts to Cadillacs at the rate of more than 500,000 per year. General Motors is on the top ten list of the largest employers in the state; and each year the auto industry makes payments to employees and local suppliers in New Jersey totaling over $600 million. Some eighty companies cater exclusively to the auto industry, from the auto plants themselves to the sheet metal stampers and fabricators for car bodies; from the parts manufacturers for brakes, batteries, clutches, and ball bearings, to the plastic extruders for dashboards and other interior features. Hundreds of other companies devote some part of their business to the automobile industry.

All of this economic activity, along with the suburban character of many parts of the state, has created a car culture in New Jersey that is in many ways as rich as California's, if not as renowned. The commercial development of highways like Routes 1, 9, 17, 18, and 22 is awesome in its density and diversity. In a half-hour drive on Route 22 east from Somerville you can see fast-food joints, restaurants serving American, Italian, and Chinese food, eyeglass centers, carpet stores, furniture warehouses, stereo shops, department stores, motels, gas stations, new and used car lots, movie theaters, shoe stores, a newspaper building, an amusement park, a company that makes burial vaults, and, of course, New Jersey's eatery *par excellence:* the twenty-four-hour diner. In fact, there are virtually no diners accessible by mass transit — certainly not at night or on weekends, when most buses and trains stop running. The diner — like another great New Jersey institution, the shopping center — grew up with the car.

There are more than four million cars registered in the state, and on a summer Saturday morning it looks like they are all headed south on the Garden State Parkway to the shore. In 1979 the state transportation department tried to persuade beachcombers to take the train by introducing low weekend fares and free bus service from the station to the beach. But the effort failed. People who travel in New Jersey still think in terms of exit numbers, not timetables. The landscape is defined by overpasses, ramps, jughandles, traffic circles, driveways, yield signs, and gas stations.

So many of the quintessential New Jersey pursuits — the experiences that are more New Jersey, and more richly New Jersey, than anything else — are bound up with the culture and cult of the car. Flea markets, those parking lots turned bazaars, are legendary in New Jersey. One of them, the Englishtown Auction Sales, claims to be the largest flea market in the world — and anyone who has driven there early on a weekend morning would be hard put to deny it. The trip, from home garage to cacophonous marketplace, is something of a pilgrimage, replete with mystical experiences in the traffic jam at 6 A.M. New Jersey also abounds in roadside fruit and vegetable stands, which thrive on regular customers who drive past every day on their way home from work, as well as shore-bound vacationers who zip by, catch the gleam of corn and tomato, and screech to a stop. The first drive-in movie was built in Camden in 1933, and the institution has been going strong in New Jersey ever since. Palatial shopping malls, with their oceanic parking lots, have risen and prospered throughout the state. And every summer, cars from throughout the Northeast flock to Great Adventure, the drive-through safari park and amusement complex in rural Jackson.

New Jersey has a large and enthusiastic antique car following. One of the largest antique car shows on the East Coast is the New Hope Auto Show: about 1,000 cars, both antiques and classics, are displayed. There are New Jersey chapters of all the large antique car clubs, the oldest and largest being the Antique Auto Club of America, with some 1,000 members in New Jersey. Small shows of ten to 100 cars are held every weekend in the state, from spring thaw to the first snowfall. Serving this subculture is a highly skilled community of artisan-mechanics who specialize in antique car restoration. For these perfectionists, bliss means one thing: a fine old automobile lovingly returned to its original splendor.

New Jerseyans also love to watch cars race. There are popular drag racing tracks in Englishtown, Collingswood, Great Meadows, and Trenton. At Englishtown, a normal weeknight drag race will draw 10,000 spectators. And every summer the National Hot Rod Association holds a national meet in Englishtown, to which 40,000 fans swarm. The world's record for acceleration, according to the *Guinness Book of World Records,* is held by Sam "Slam'n Sammy" Miller of Wayne. Miller zoomed from a dead stop to 360 miles per hour in 3.94 seconds.

Nothing so embodies car culture, however, or so graphi- cally defines New Jersey's national image as a car-cultured state, as the New Jersey Turnpike. It is probably the most famous road in America. It is a myth, the subject of song, poetry, movies, and contemporary folk tales. Angus K. Gillespie, an American Studies professor and folklorist at Rutgers, calls the Turnpike "a symbol, icon, and metaphor of American culture." Where else, after all, can you find a service area named after Vince Lombardi?

Starting in the south, just this side of the Delaware Memorial Bridge, in Salem County, the Turnpike courses through the countryside like any interstate, a four-lane highway with rural vistas and occasional glimpses of housing developments. Toward Hightstown, a few industrial plants appear. But it is after Exit 9, the New Brunswick interchange, that the Turnpike comes into its own. The highway widens — in a grand, muscular gesture — to twelve lanes, six for cars alone and six for cars, trucks, buses, and any other earth-bound creature on wheels. This is no mere artery; it is the vehicular aorta, the trunk line carrying life stuff to the entire body. All is motion here, and in the universal drone of tires on pavement, upon the vast acreage of tempered asphalt, divided only by painted lines and the thin strips of guard rail, all sojourners are equal. All men are cars.

North beyond Exit 11 (the Garden State Parkway-Woodbridge interchange), the Turnpike surges through the industrial heartland of New Jersey, the looming macabre metalscape of clustered round tanks and towers spewing fire. Entering upon this region, one recalls that life began in some tidal pool where chemicals married, and one wonders what strange elemental forces mingle here — and what life they will spawn. Northward still, deafening roars envelop the roadway, as airplanes belly down over the cars on their approach to Newark Airport. The Turnpike ends with visions of New York, on the threshold of the George Washington Bridge.

It is a nation unto itself, the Turnpike, with its own boundaries — 141.5 miles in length, including various extensions and spurs — its own census — 121 million vehicles in 1979 — and its own budget — $100 million in tolls that same year. An entire troop of state police, 171 strong, patrols the Turnpike, with a fleet of ninety-eight marked cars, three radar vans, and an undisclosed number of unmarked cars. Four mechanics work full-time to maintain this fleet, which nevertheless wears out and is replaced every year. (Municipal police forces get the cast-offs.) On an average day the Turnpike police respond to 250 calls for help, from flat tires to overheated engines to empty gas tanks.

Some people hate the Turnpike, and some love it. Some find it repulsive, some boring, some awe-inspiring. To many strangers, including some who have never seen New Jersey, the Turnpike defines the state. Even natives often describe where they live by citing the nearest Turnpike exit. And there is something fitting in that. Who has not emerged from a toll plaza to confront, with the exhilarating freedom of the traveler, that primal choice: North or South? Who has not had a breakdown between exits and been towed from the secure, familiar surroundings of the road to the wilderness of an alien city's garage? Who has not sped, unawares, into the fog-bound lowlands late at night and crept forth, relieved, at his home exit? The Turnpike is, above all, a center of our shared experience. It is our Broadway. It is our Brooklyn Bridge.

— *Paul Bradley*

Twenty-four hours a day, all twelve lanes of the New Jersey Turnpike are alive with cars. One of the safest major highways in the country, shown here looking south toward Elizabeth, it has been called "a symbol, icon, and metaphor of American culture."

With only a few miles on their odometers, new Mercedes and BMWs stream off the docks of Port Elizabeth.

Overleaf: These taut filaments of light are actually cars coursing through the north tube of the Lincoln Tunnel, shown here in a time exposure.

In the picturesque Bergen County Village of Ridgewood, as in the big city, automobiles are an essential part of life.

All sales are final at this hubcap shop in Newark, a business which reflects New Jersey's unique car culture.

In a prank reminiscent of the fifties, sixteen students at the Lawrenceville School, one of the top preparatory schools in America, crowd into a 1959 Buick.

Right: Every summer, vacationers from throughout the Northeast flock to Great Adventure in Jackson, where a giraffe loping alongside a visitor's car is a desired, rather than disconcerting, experience.

Overleaf: Amateur and professional dirtbikers participate in the thrilling motocross event at Englishtown's Raceway Park.

A gleaming expanse of used cars fills the lot of Garron Motors in Vineland.

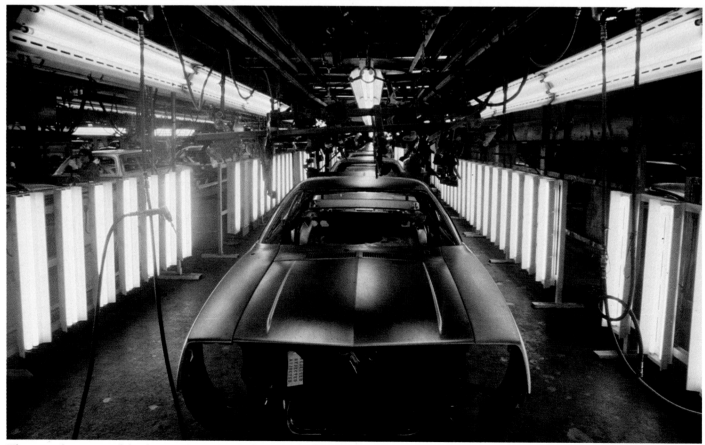

There are four automobile plants in New Jersey; here, at Ford's Edison location, subcompact Pintos are born by the thousands.

Opposite: A study in incongruity: Patrolling the grounds of Raceway Park, a husky Englishtown policeman stops to rest on his tiny Honda moped.

COMMUNICATIONS

Photographs by Bob Krist

TIPPED TOWARD THE HEAVENS, THREE giant white saucers are perched on a hillside in northwestern New Jersey. These satellite antennas, silent and powerful, are turning the quiet valley of ski slopes and dairy farms into a major communications center.

It is a simple matter of geography that prompted RCA to build its satellite communications earth station in the Vernon Valley. It is geography that prompted Western Union and American Satellite Corporation to do the same. For the Vernon Valley is the first "radio quiet" area outside of New York City.

"The ridge over there that makes such nice ski slopes also provides radio interference protection from the New York metropolitan area," says RCA station manager Archie Miller, pointing toward the manicured slopes of Playboy's Great Gorge resort. "So this rural area out here has become a pivotal point in communications."

It is a story that has repeated itself over and over. Located next door to the largest city in the United States, New Jersey has become a communications hub because of geography and convenience.

In part, it was the need for open spaces that led scientists to leave New York and cross the Hudson in the early part of the century. Those interested in radio also found the flat coastal plains of the New Jersey shore ideally suited to radio transmissions. Thus radio grew up in New Jersey. Guglielmo Marconi constructed one of the first transatlantic radio tow-

ers in New Brunswick, and Amelia Earhart's airplane was outfitted with ground-to-air radio at a Bell Laboratories facility in Whippany. Radio astronomy was born in Holmdel in the 1930s, and the transistor was invented at Bell Labs in 1947.

Next came color TV, invented by RCA in the late forties, and the laser, which was developed by Bell Labs in the sixties. Research today is continuing on such exotic projects as "talking" computers and "smart" telephones.

The beginnings, however, were modest, even for the forerunners of the giant Bell System. In 1920, Western Electric scientist Walter Friis began his work on shortwave radio in a shack in Elberon. His desk was a board and two packing cases, and his job was to study and measure radio reception from ships. By 1926, a small field station had been built in Whippany, and in 1930 a building called "The Turkey Farm" was built by the Labs in Holmdel for investigation of shortwave radio communications.

Today New Jersey is headquarters to the entire Bell System. With the American Telephone & Telegraph Company in Basking Ridge, Long Lines in Bedminster, Western Electric in Newark, and seven Bell Labs outposts across the state, Ma Bell is the largest employer in New Jersey. More than 40,000 people work for the Bell System in the state, not to mention the 30,000 more employed by the local phone company, New Jersey Bell.

The Long Lines facility by itself would be enough to put

New Jersey on the communications map. It is here that the country's top telephone managers continually design and redesign the nation's telephone network. Sitting in a control center that resembles a military war room, these managers make decisions that determine how every phone call in the country will be routed. A giant board monitors switching stations throughout the United States, and the impact of a natural disaster is likely to show up on the network transmission map before it is reported on the TV news.

The state also plays a key role in the operations of other communications giants. RCA, for example, has its principal research labs in Princeton, a space center in Hightstown, a computer controlled telex exchange in Piscataway, and a solid state technology center in Somerville.

It is Bell Labs, however, that has made New Jersey the gathering place for the nation's communications elite. With seven of sixteen Bell Labs facilities located in the state, virtually every piece of telephone equipment in the country can be traced in some way to New Jersey. Owned jointly by AT&T and Western Electric (the Bell System's manufacturing arm), Bell Labs provides a hothouse environment for physicists, biologists, chemists, psychologists, engineers, and mathematicians. With an annual budget of $1 billion and a staff that includes more than 2,400 Ph.Ds, its stated purpose is to develop a more advanced telephone network.

Inevitably, though, the research has led to discoveries that transcend improved phone service. Development of the transistor started the electronics revolution, which is making the computer a household item; invention of the laser led to new surgical techniques; and, most recently, the discovery of noise from the far reaches of space confirmed "The Big Bang" theory of the origin of the universe.

Bell Labs facilities are also visible proof that technology is profitable. From the sprawling yellow brick headquarters in Murray Hill to the shiny reflective glass laboratories in Holmdel, the buildings that house Bell Labs scientists are statements of corporate success.

Less visible, however, is the fact that these massive buildings can't keep pace with the communications explosion. They are running out of space. Bell Labs no longer has room for all of the administrative personnel in Murray Hill, and the impressive Holmdel facility is already being expanded. Even the brand new Long Lines headquarters was too small by the time it was completed in 1977: nearly 200 employees had to be housed in rented office space.

Perhaps the most dramatic growth will be in the quiet Vernon Valley, where the future of domestic satellite communications is just beginning to unfold. Already the RCA earth station is in the midst of hasty expansion in preparation for the launch of two new satellites in 1981. In addition to providing satellite hookups for the New York metropolitan area, the tiny earth station will soon be responsible for helping to keep four satellites in their proper orbits. That may not seem like much of an expansion until you realize that each satellite will be able to transmit as many as 45,000 phone conversations at one time.

In 1955, RCA's David Sarnoff wrote in *Fortune* magazine, "There is no element of material progress that we know today . . . that will not seem, from the vantage point of 1980, a fumbling prelude." Those who compare the giant white saucers in the Vernon Valley with Marconi's first radio tower will see that it is still just the beginning.   — *Lynn Asinof*

Sophisticated research techniques responsible for the invention of color television continue today at Sarnoff Labs, RCA's Princeton facility.

Glowing red fiber optics, developed by Bell Labs in Murray Hill, will eventually replace copper telephone wire. They are presently used in everything from microsurgery to decorative lighting fixtures.

The control room at AT&T Long Lines' nerve center in Bedminster is dominated by a huge map, on which technicians can view telephone traffic anywhere in the United States, and route calls according to traffic conditions.

Virtually every town in the country appears on the monitoring board at AT&T, a small portion of which is pictured here.

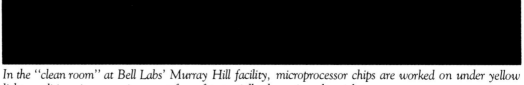

In the "clean room" at Bell Labs' Murray Hill facility, microprocessor chips are worked on under yellow light conditions in an environment free of potentially damaging ultraviolet rays.

Inset: An entire computer program can be stored on a microprocessor chip, only slightly bigger than a paper clip. Twenty years ago, it would have taken an entire warehouse to contain that much data.

ATLANTIC CITY

Photographs by Jeffrey A. Newman

JOHNNY CARSON PERFORMS THERE TO sell-out crowds. Other performers—their names and faces run on full-page ads in the Sunday *New York Times* — include David Brenner, Buddy Hackett, Steve Martin, Frank Sinatra, Johnny Cash, and Donna Summer. This is not Las Vegas or Reno, but Atlantic City. The City by the Sea has become a national showcase for big-name talent. For Atlantic City has become a national playground again, a resort that everyone knows. Casino gambling, New Jersey's controversial economic, social, and political experiment, has transformed the once dynamic, then dying shore town.

Nobody thought in the 1800s that the sand and swampland of Absecon Island would ever become a tourist resort. Well, almost nobody: Dr. Jonathan Pitney of Mendham owned 25,000 acres of the island and he had visions of a seaside mecca. In 1852 Pitney organized the Camden and Atlantic Railroad to buy land from individual owners on the island and to build a railroad from Camden to Absecon. Six hundred guests made the first trip on July 1, 1854, and the resort was born. Atlantic City officially became a city on May 1, 1855, when the city charter received formal state approval.

The population grew slowly at first, from 250 permanent residents in 1855 to only 1,000 in 1870. That was the year of the Boardwalk. During the next twenty years the population increased more than tenfold. The wooden street had a tremendous impact on the city's importance as a resort town. People from all over came to walk the Boardwalk, which at first was only ten feet wide and eighteen inches off the ground. The Boardwalk was proposed by Jacob Keim and Alexander Boardman, both hotel owners, to the local citizens in the spring of 1870. Keim and Boardman wanted to protect their furniture and rugs from the sand tracked in by patrons who were beach-walking. They figured the best way to solve their problem was to get the public off the sand and onto a wooden promenade.

The Boardwalk proved too popular. No railings had been built on either side of it, and people literally fell off trying to make their way through the crowds. Because of the heavy use and damage from storms, it had to be replaced four times in the next twenty-six years. The final, permanent Boardwalk was built in 1896 by the Phoenix Bridge Company. It was four miles long, forty feet wide, and several feet up off the beach.

Atlantic City flourished through World War II, hosting not only entertainers but also conventions, pageants (the Miss America Pageant being the most famous, of course), all manner of arcade-style amusements, assorted frivolities, and lots of family fun. Then, gradually, began the decline. It is not that the city aged, but that it didn't: it remained more or less the same, while the world got younger. Its *style* — that fine old style, classy but generous, democratic — this is what aged. The world passed on to newer diversions while Atlantic City remained Atlantic City — and then ebbed, losing itself, losing what it had been. As the post-war era advanced, Atlantic City became less exotic to pleasure-seekers. The jet plane made spots like Miami Beach and the Bahamas more accessible. For the rich, Atlantic City no longer represented someplace distant and enticing.

The legalization of casino gambling in 1976 was a turning point. In two dramatic strokes — the statewide referendum and the enabling legislation — a new industry, a contemporary industry, was born in New Jersey. Money flowed in — private money from big companies. Real estate values shot up, causing social displacement and making new millionaires. And construction began, construction the likes of which Atlantic City had not seen in a long time. Instantaneously, it seemed, blocks were razed, fences went up, and girders sprouted. Before long, Resorts International opened the doors of its casino — to mobs. Caesar's World followed with the Boardwalk Regency, and Bally's Park Place came next. All over town, meanwhile, signs proclaimed: "Coming Soon . . . Coming Soon . . ." A city cannot absorb such sudden change without some convulsions. There have been plenty of controversies in the resurgent resort. But there is life in Atlantic City, of the sort there used to be. Atlantic City is on the map again. Atlantic City is . . .Atlantic City.

— *Paul Bradley*

MEADOWLANDS

Photographs by Klaus Schnitzer

THERE IS A CITIZEN OF NEW JERSEY known to many as, simply, "The Man Who Water-skis The Hackensack." He navigates the river in that mercurial region known as the Meadowlands, skidding along as if in humble pursuit of the cars and trucks and trailers that forge past him on the Turnpike. A dwarfed and anonymous sportsman. The boat that pulls him sets out from the Harmon Cove Marina, in an inlet of larger and smaller vessels surrounded by wooden, rusticated townhouses in which the skier presumably lives. Once upriver, he passes on the east bank the Meadowlands Hilton, from whose pool deck he can be watched in graceful chase, and Harmon Tower, a ten-story office building of reflecting glass. Behind it, just in view, are the Harmon Cove Quadracinema and the Tiger Racquet Club. On the opposite bank, slightly further up, he comes to what has been repeatedly called "the most versatile sports and entertainment center in the country" — that sprawling complex that includes Giants Stadium, home of football's Giants and soccer's Cosmos; The Meadowlands Race Track, serving both harness and thoroughbred racing, and now the home of the Hambletonian, harness racing's Kentucky Derby; and Meadowlands Arena, which will house the basketball Nets and, it is hoped, a franchise in hockey. Yet despite this cornucopia of professionalism, the lonely water-skier taking his liquidy constitutional is, if less heralded, no less appreciated. He is watched from, among other points, the seventh floor of Harmon Tower, where Eugene Heller, president of Hartz Mountain Industries, not only awaits his

habitual passage, like that familiar routine without which a day is not complete, but boasts of it, as that living proof that his dream has been achieved.

"People don't believe that someone water-skis on the Hackensack River," says Heller. "They'd say a few years ago you didn't have to ski, you could have walked across it. But the river's been cleaned up. I've seen the guy fall in a few times. He comes up all right. And he's not green all over."

Heller's distinct preoccupation with green stems from an experience he had in 1969. It was then that he convinced Hartz Mountain chairman Leonard Stern to buy 700 acres of the Meadowlands for $10 million. Showing him the site proved somewhat embarrassing. There is one version of the story that has a group of men, visionary developers, slowly, slowly sinking as they plot and plan their kingdom. "And there will be the industrial park . . . plop, plop, plop . . . and here the . . . plop, plop, plop . . . office tower." Heller says simply, "I just walked out too far and sank up to my waist in green slime."

In New Jersey's rich and varied regional nomenclature, "Meadowlands" is one of the most confounding terms. The Meadowlands are more accurately a 19,730-acre saltwater marsh. In the early days, an enterprising few tried to turn the area into genuine meadowlands, in hopes of wealth derived from selling dairy products to New York, but the dikes they had to build sank and their "meadows" once again became flooded. The land was left idle save for maverick muskrat hunters, pig farms, and unsightly garbage dumps.

When Hartz Mountain purchased its share of the land, the company intended to construct only warehousing and distribution facilities, primarily for those firms that, through lack of money or space, were being excluded from New York. But in the meantime, the Hackensack Meadowlands Development Commission had been established and with it a master plan for land use that called for, among other things, residential developments. Heller and Stern doubted at first whether people would want to live in the Meadowlands, and immediately found their worries unfounded. People flocked to live there. The townhouses of Harmon Cove I and II were finished in 1977, offering 640 units that were readily filled. A marina of 40 slips was included, and it, too, was quickly filled — with everything from sailboats to power boats. Other recreational amenities added to the allure: The Tiger Racquet Club contained health facilities, racquetball courts, and nine tennis courts under a high, almost unreachable roof, constructed, it is said, to accommodate Heller's well-honed lob. Outdoor tennis courts were added, along with swimming pools, a softball field, four movie theaters in one building, and, of course, the Meadowlands Hilton, with its 312 rooms, indoor-outdoor swimming pools, restaurants, ballrooms, and exhibition center. New, high-rise condominiums are next up as neighbors to Harmon Cove, with facilities such as steam and exercise rooms, saunas, tennis courts, and a two-and-a-half-mile jogging path along the riverfront. It seems conceivable that because there is so much to do here, one may forget about the spectating across the way.

Yet the Sports Complex, under the authoritative name of the New Jersey Sports and Exposition Authority, has surely not suffered. If anything, it has gained. In 1979 fifty-two events were held in Giants Stadium, attended by 2.2 million fans. Both of the stadium's teams, the Giants and the Cosmos, led their leagues in attendance. Over at the racetrack, they watched more than four and a half million people come in during this same year, including 41,155 for the opening night of the thoroughbred season. And there is money here apart from tickets and concessions — in 1979 more than $582 million was wagered at the track.

The Sports Complex grew up, and is still growing, without a defined form. Its chief rule of expansion is "Necessity (especially in the clubhouses of New York) is the mother of construction." It began back in the early 1970s when it became known that the New York Yankees were looking for a new home in which to play baseball. David A. (Sonny) Werblin, then chairman of the Authority, negotiated. The Yankees, as is now known, dropped out of the discussions, but the New York Giants became involved. The Giants, who had never had their own stadium, were promised it in the Meadowlands: an arena bearing their name (something which, in the case of the Yankees, would have bordered on plagiarism), and, perhaps unknown, if not unimportant to them, decorated in their team colors — red and blue.

Because Giants Stadium was built specifically for them, it is said to be one of the finest places to watch, and consequently to play, football in the country. No space was allowed for such sundry stadium regulars as track or baseball diamond, enabling the seats (all 78,000 of them) to give directly onto the field. The angles at which the seats rise are incredibly sharp, creating advantageous sightlines and a sense, as commentators love to say, of "being on top of the action." It was the first stadium in the country to have two video-matrix computerized scoreboards — both of which can give, along with the usual niceties of downs and yards to go, images of the athletes, twenty-five feet high, and instant replay. When neither the Giants nor the Cosmos are using it, the stadium can be, and has been, used for everything from college football to college graduations, artful antique shows, and antic rock concerts.

The money to finance the stadium was conveniently provided by the racetrack. "This is the uniqueness of the complex," explains Robert E. Mulcahy III, Executive Director of the New Jersey Sports and Exposition Authority. "There is no other complex in the country that uses a racetrack as the key financial vehicle." As much as it has helped the stadium, it has not done badly itself. It is now considered the greatest harness track in the world, judged on the three essentials of purses, attendance, and quality of horses. The Hambletonian was awarded it on these grounds, and Mulcahy looks to that event with a great sense of pride. He calls it "acquiring tradition." In addition, a night in the track's Pegasus Restaurant is regarded by many as a class date.

The Meadowlands is still a paradoxical name for this once beleaguered, now be-leagued, region of the state. Its success is not incomprehensible when one realizes that within one hour's driving time live eighteen million people. And many of those are sports-crazed denizens of a state long lacking in professional games. "The complex has brought a new sense of pride to the people of New Jersey," states Mulcahy. "For one thing it is the number one sports complex in the country. And for another, you don't have to cross a river any more."

— *Thomas Swick*

In the Meadowlands, vistas of grassy marsh provide a sharp contrast to Giants Stadium, the cornerstone of the new Sports Complex.

Townhouse dwellers in Harmon Cove laze around a pool. It is one of the many recreational amenities offered at this 640-unit residential development in the Meadowlands.

Hartz Mountain Industrial Park in Secaucus is the home of many top-quality clothing outlets, a fashion-conscious bargain hunter's paradise.

The World War II submarine S.S. Ling is on permanent display at the edge of the Meadowlands, in Hackensack.

Diners at Pegasus can enjoy gourmet fare in an elegant setting while viewing the action below at the world's greatest harness track.

The Meadowlands Hilton plays host to people from all over the country. Overleaf: A country and western concert at Giants Stadium.

HEADQUARTERS

Photographs by Allan Weitz

THE LOOK IS MANICURED. THE GRASS IS uniformly clipped, the trees are flawlessly placed, and there is not a single brown leaf curling among the perfect pink azaleas. Every detail has been considered, and the psychological impact is impressive.

They could be exclusive country clubs or perhaps college campuses. Yet beneath their understated elegance, New Jersey's corporate headquarters are places of power. Neither rain nor snow disturbs the harmony of the multi-tiered edifices that reign over the New Jersey countryside in increasing numbers.

There is American Telephone & Telegraph Company's new headquarters in Basking Ridge, unquestionably one of the most impressive tributes to corporate power. Sloping Oriental roofs and terraced architecture soften the lines of the massive building, and the effect is that of Kublai Khan's castle nestled in the New Jersey countryside.

Yet AT&T is only one of dozens. In fact, more than forty of the Fortune 1,000 are headquartered in the state, and surveys show that New Jersey now rivals New York as the state most often considered for a corporate relocation.

Already New Jersey is home to American Cyanamid, Bell Telephone Laboratories, Campbell Soup, Western Union, A&P, Lenox, the David Sarnoff Research Center of RCA Laboratories, Federal Paper Board, and Ingersoll-Rand.

Opposite: The Mercedes-Benz logo is echoed in the facade of its imposing hexagonal headquarters building in Montvale.

There is Union Camp Corporation's wooded headquarters site in Wayne, the sweeping lines of Nabisco's concrete and glass structure in East Hanover, and the campus environment of Allied Chemical Corporation's 151-acre headquarters in Morris Township.

Built on former golf courses and old estates, the headquarters are designed to project an image of taste and quality. E. R. Squibb & Sons' glass and brick jewel, for example, sits above a twelve-acre lake on 273 acres of former farmland in Princeton. More than 2,000 trees, 11,000 shrubs, and 181,000 plants cover the grounds and roof gardens of the drug company's world headquarters. Yet with the exception of a single baseball diamond, the grounds are ornamental, used mainly by flocks of migrating ducks and geese.

The inside of the building is landscaped, too — with roof-high schefflera trees arching over a splashing fountain and delicate Boston ferns banking the lobby. The lush interior is echoed by carefully planted gardens outside the tinted glass walls, and everywhere something green is growing.

Such studied beauty, however, is only for those who can afford it. Built in 1971, Squibb's world headquarters and research center cost $22 million. Although Squibb views the seven-building complex as a good investment, corporate officers admit that it would be difficult to construct identical facilities in 1980.

AT&T Long Lines' sprawling white headquarters in Bedminster, just down the road from its parent company in Basking Ridge, was completed in 1977 at a cost of $65 million. Described as a thirty-five-story high-rise lying on its side, the project includes a computerized energy-saving system, water quality monitoring on the Raritan River, and a new sewage treatment plant. Special construction techniques were even used to save more than 100 trees on the 422-acre site.

Despite such increased costs, corporations continue to view New Jersey as a prime headquarters location. Those who spend their time courting the corporations say the decision to relocate is an economic one, but the choice of location is prompted by more mundane factors. Most important, they say, is where the chairman of the board lives.

The general pattern is for downtown New York City companies to cross the Hudson River, since much of their work force commutes on PATH trains. Midtown corporations tend to look north along the rail lines to Westchester County and Connecticut. More than one conglomerate, however, has chosen the northeastern part of New Jersey to accommodate chief executives who live in Connecticut, where there is no state income tax.

While the location is determined by the corporate brass, the building is usually designed for the employees. Since most new headquarters are built on isolated sites in suburban communities, employees don't often run errands on their lunch hour or even go out to lunch. As a result, companies build special facilities designed to make the corporate campus a self-contained community.

As one employer explained, "When you are out in the suburbs you must do everything you can to enhance the area. After all, the employee has no place to go. He's committed to staying in the area for a period of eight or nine hours. So it helps to have a country club atmosphere."

The Liggett Group in Montvale, for example, has a full gymnasium at its corporate headquarters. At CPC International in Englewood Cliffs, patio furniture is arranged around the reflecting pool in the summer, and a company store carries everything from Mother's Day cards to panty hose. Movies are shown at Long Lines, and Squibb sponsors art exhibits in its specially designed art gallery. Most importantly, all offer subsidized lunches in a variety of settings ranging from self-service cafeterias to posh dining rooms.

The country club atmosphere, however, hasn't dented the corporate ranking system that dictates everything from the size of the offices to the style of their furnishings. At CPC, for example, offices are graded A to D, with the largest measuring 30 by 15 feet and the smallest one-third that size. The corner offices at Squibb are reserved for vice-presidents, while at Long Lines the vice-presidents get windowed offices on the fourth floor.

For despite the art galleries, the beautiful plantings, and the magnificent architecture, these buildings are designed for business. So there is something beautifully straightforward about the fact that Squibb's technical library is en route to a lakeside cafeteria and that the gurgling fountain in the lobby gives privacy to any conversation.

These glorious edifices were built to impress, but the most impressive thing about them is that they work.

— *Lynn Asinof*

130 employees work in the Lenox China Company's exquisite white building in Lawrenceville.

Opposite: Two employees stroll through the glass-roofed corridor of the Thomas & Betts Corporation headquarters in Elizabeth.

The magnificently landscaped headquarters of A&P, also known as The Great Atlantic and Pacific Tea Company, were completed in 1973.

At Federal Paper Board executive offices in Montvale, 150 employees administer the manufacture and sale of pulp, paperboard, and lumber.

The Liggett Group in Montvale has built a full gymnasium and other creature comforts on the premises.

An intricate neon ceiling illuminates the lengthy entrance tunnel of American Cyanamid's headquarters in Bound Brook.

The sloping Oriental roof and terraced architecture of
AT&T's corporate headquarters in Basking Ridge give the effect of
a pagoda nestled in the New Jersey countryside.

Fiat is one of fifteen foreign car companies which have established their corporate headquarters in New Jersey.

This picturesque courtyard, complete with fountains, provides workers at CPC International with an idyllic setting for alfresco lunches.

Opposite: The new Bell Labs complex in Holmdel is already being expanded to accommodate the growing number of physicists, biologists, chemists, psychologists, and mathematicians working on an ever expanding telephone network.

In the elegantly designed lobby of BMW North America, the company's latest models of luxury cars are displayed for visitors and employees.

Benjamin Moore & Company in Montvale is one of the country's largest manufacturers of paints, enamels, and varnishes.

Opposite: The sky is never out of sight in the lobby of E. R. Squibb & Sons, a pharmaceutical company with headquarters in Princeton.

The Union Camp Corporation headquarters building stands at the edge of a reflecting pond.

The Ingersoll Rand Company's Woodcliff Lake location houses over 300 employees in this angular contemporary structure.

Opposite: Nabisco Inc. in East Hanover hosts many art exhibits, providing employees with cultural stimulation in a working environment.

The Haines & Haines Cranberry Farm in Chatsworth is veiled in a tranquil October mist.

CRANBERRIES

Photographs by Michael Spozarsky

PINE BARRENS WAS THE NAME GIVEN the sandy, woody expanse of land in the south of New Jersey by the first settlers, but with only partial precision. For while no one can deny the overwhelming presence of pine — great stretches of green and oft-times charred pitch pine under a blue summer sky; long vistas of dwarf pine undulating across the flat sandy earth; seemingly endless forests of pine, interrupted only by lost mazes of sand roads and a few thin slips of black macadam — there are many who would dispute the notion of barrenness. For one thing, this realm of pine lies over, and helps protect, an immense reservoir of pure water, one of the largest natural water recharging sites in the world. And, on a less grandiose scale, the Pines have been a source of legend: here, in these uncharted woods, is where the Jersey Devil was first rumored to roam. This fabulous beast, our state's own beloved Loch Ness monster, has been described as "a leather-winged, steel-springed jumper of goat size that could clear a cranberry bog at a bound." John McPhee, one of the country's foremost nonfiction writers (and a longtime New Jersey resident) found the nominally barren Pinelands rich enough to write a book about them. In *The Pine Barrens*, which has become a small classic, McPhee marveled at the very existence of the Pines in an era of growing urban congestion. Surveying the view from Bear Swamp Hill, he wrote: "The picture of New Jersey that most people hold in their minds is so different from this one that, considered beside it, the Pine Barrens, as they are called, become as incongruous as they are beautiful. . . . New Jersey has nearly a thousand people per square mile — the greatest population density of any state in the Union. . . . In the central area of the Pine Barrens — the forest land that is still so undeveloped that it can be called wilderness — there are only fifteen people per square mile." And though it is a land most often seen in summer — traversed by vacationers between city and shore — it is one most evident in winter. For every Christmas our homes become showcases for the products of the Pines: candle holders made from their birch trees; pine cones picked by their pineballers; wreaths arranged of pitch pine, holly, laurel, and mistletoe; and delights both decorative and edible made from that gustatory jewel of our wintry feasts — cranberry.

The cranberry (*Vaccinium macrocarpon*) is, along with the blueberry, one of America's few truly native fruits. It is a low-lying evergreen vine that puts out two types of growth: the runner, or vegetative type, and the upshoot, or reproductive type. The upshoot flowers sometime in June in pale, pink blossoms that tend to resemble a crane in appearance — hence the original name "craneberry," shortened over the years to cranberry. After pollination, berries are produced. The Indians used the cranberry in poultices for their wounds and also mixed it in hopeful doses as a preservative for meats. According to legend, the Pilgrims of Plymouth were given venison garnished with cranberries as a gift of friendship.

The early settlers in the Pine Barrens found cranberries growing wild, as on Cape Cod. These people were of an assorted mix: Welshmen, Englishmen, Scots, Frenchmen, and Germans — among these lapsed Quakers and deserting Hessians, tarred Tories and homesick Huguenots. And in all fairness to their perspicacity, their new homeland did seem, at first — and often even at second — glance, less than fruitful. The crops they tried fared miserably, and it was only fitting that they harvested the cranberries growing in the wilds all about them with a mocking ease. These were the sorts of labors that in retrospect appear so idyllic — classes let out early so schoolchildren could gather with their masters, and mothers worked all day in sunbonnets and aprons of oilcloth stained a brilliant red. After the work there were games; berries were threaded on a needle for a necklace, with the fastest threaders awarded the honor of placing the jewelry on their sweethearts for a kiss. But there was no way to make a living from these pursuits, so the men employed themselves mostly as ironworkers, cabinetmakers, or smugglers.

Of those three trades, the last is perennially unstable, while the first, which supported the second, was by the mid-1800s, in the Pine Barrens, moribund. The coal and iron ore finds in western Pennsylvania eclipsed the bog iron industry in the Pines. But at the same time, on the edge of Burr's Mill Pond in Southampton Township, a new bog-bound industry was begun.

Benjamin Thomas was the first man in New Jersey to cultivate the cranberry, taking the vines of the wild plants and caring for them in nearby bogs. He found, along with others soon to follow — people like "Old Peg Leg" John Webb and William Braddock — that the soil of the Pine Barrens was ideal for the cranberry's growth. The sensitive, capricious cranberry needs a highly acidic soil of peaty and sandy composition, with an abundance of pure water close to the surface — the natural conditions of the Pines.

By the 1860s there was a veritable "cranberry craze" in New Jersey, which evolved far beyond the original, pioneering family farms. Not only in the Pine Barrens of Burlington County, but in Cape May, Atlantic, Monmouth, Gloucester, Camden, Middlesex, Ocean, Mercer, and even Sussex counties, bogs were born. Slogans of "Buy a Bog" were bandied about in the advertisements of northeastern cities. On the one hand, it was as inexplicable as any craze; on the other, there was a sensible connection to the cranberry's nutritional benefits. For on the long ocean voyages of this time, before refrigeration, the crews needed a source of Vitamin C that would not spoil in passage. The tart cranberry was found to suit, if not their tastes, their needs. Between 1875 and 1885 production increased ten times over. In 1885 Joseph J. White of Whitesbog (whose daughter was to become equally expert in blueberry circles), published a book titled *Cranberry Culture* that, some years later, was described as "the Bible of American cranberry growers."

The culture prospered until about 1916, when, though the vines grew and the flowers bloomed, no berries appeared. The cause was found to be a virus infection, which was termed "the false blossom virus." The disease was spread by the blunt-nosed cranberry leaf hopper, destined to become a Jersey Devil in its own right. This disaster devastated the cranberry industry. Hundreds of growers deserted their bogs, others turned them into blueberry fields, and almost half of the original number of counties ceased production.

Along with the problems of growing, there were problems of marketing. However useful as a source of Vitamin C, the cranberry *qua* cranberry had never exactly endeared itself to the tasting public. *The New York Times* has described it as "a lowly Indian berry with limited natural demand and a flavor that, unadulterated, could raise blisters on asbestos." As success stories go, this one is not without its improbability. One day in the town of New Egypt, in the late 1920s, Elizabeth C. Lee gathered the cranberries her brother was about to discard for lack of clients. She cooked them into a jelly and sealed the jelly into jars. With eight full cases she traveled to Philadelphia, to one of the city's largest department stores, and asked to see the food buyer. When he appeared and heard of her concoction and her desire to market it, he suggested that she might be crazy. She explained that, no, she was rather an old woman and too frail to carry the cases back with her to New Jersey. She would leave them, she said, without payment, if the buyer agreed at least to taste their contents. She returned to New Egypt and several days later received a call from the buyer, who ordered 500 cases for the coming year. Such were the beginnings of cranberry sauce.

In time, the virus was virtually eradicated and nothing was to influence the cultivation of cranberries in New Jersey so profoundly until the 1960s, when, with a much more positive effect, the method of wet harvesting was introduced. William Haines Sr. of Hogs Wallow brought the principle, and the machine, to the Pine Barrens from Cape Cod. At this time most of the harvesting in the Pines was done with wooden scoops — heavy, hand-driven, many-teethed tools that combed the vines, cutting off the berries from their dangles. It was an inefficient system in that it not only tore up a lot of the vines, but it also let fall a good number of berries underfoot. For years, Haines, along with John Lee of Chatsworth, had harvested these "salvage floats" by flooding the bogs after harvesting and running a small floater boat across the surface, making enough ripple through the water that the vines swayed and released the fallen berries to float slowly to the top. It took decades, though, to realize that the entire harvest could be done similarly.

Now every fall, starting in late September, the bogs are flooded, and laborers wade chest-deep through them, propelling water-pickers, which shake the berries free to swim to the surface in rich red profusions. One grower has called this harvest "the prettiest scene in the temperate zone."

But to judge by the statistics following upon the widespread use of water harvesting in New Jersey, it seems to have been almost as destructive as the virus. Mechanization in agriculture, while increasing efficiency, almost always takes its human toll, driving out of business those who cannot afford the new machines or the greater quantities of land and production that the machines demand. Moreover, the 1960s saw the amount of farmland and the number of farms in New Jersey dwindle, as more and more farmers sold out to housing developments — or occasionally to neighboring farmers. Today there are fewer cranberry growers, producing more cranberries, than there were before the advent of water harvesting. The number of growers has diminished from 475 to 50. The number of acres in cultivation has fallen from 13,000 to 3,500. The number of participating counties has decreased from nine to two. Yet the number of barrels of berries produced has risen from 90,000 to 250,000 annually, making New Jersey third behind Wisconsin and Massachusetts in total production in the country.

This has had the effect of making the remaining cranberry farmers, who invariably dabble in blueberries as well, a unique and individualistic breed. They are very often the sons and grandsons of cranberry farmers, a circumstance that is all the more inescapable today, as the land needed to farm is otherwise unobtainable. (Aside from the land needed for direct cultivation, a farmer must have supplies of sand for his bogs, wood for his dikes, and water for flooding — not only at harvest, but for winter frost prevention. Cranberry farmers are said to be the greatest water conservationists in the Pines, and not bad with land either. Indeed, their small, tight fraternity, holding zealously to its land, deserves some of the credit for keeping vast sections of the Pines free of housing developments.) But aside from land, there is the eclectic background the farmer must acquire, through many stages and many seasons, for it is said that to be a successful cranberry grower "you need to be a farmer, a hydraulics engineer, a labor relations expert, a shrewd businessman, and a hard worker."

Before the days of specialization, cranberry farmers were renowned as boastful men, who exaggerated the dimensions of their fruits with an indifference to truth that would put anglers to shame. The contemporary grower has nothing of this bombast; his is a quietly proud, self-satisfying toil with a crop that is his own, on a land he cherishes. And when asked the figures of his total acreage, he is apt, through modesty or unconcern, to forget the present sum.

Almost all of the state's growers belong to Ocean Spray Cranberries Inc., a cooperative that is a continuation of growers' organizations stretching back to Mrs. Lee's fateful trip to Philadelphia. They have taken this fruit, inedible in raw form, and made it marketable in every other form imaginable — from the common, popular cranberry sauce to such exotica as "Cranicot" juice and "Squeeze and Season" cooking sauce. Still, pickers in the Pines sometimes develop a taste for it in its natural state, and other, more benighted gourmets, have given it a try. Joseph White tells this tale in his book *Cranberry Culture:*

"A story is related of an Englishman who, upon receiving a barrel of cranberries from a friend in America, acknowledged the receipt of them, stating that 'the berries arrived safely, but they soured on the passage.' We are left to infer that the uncooked fruit was served up in cream, a mode not approved of in New Jersey."   — *Thomas Swick*

You might expect the Jersey Devil to spring from this Pine Barrens bog. Instead, the lovely marshland yields berries rich in Vitamin C.

Above: A water-picker, or beater, is used to shake the berries from their vines to float to the surface of the bog.

After the 700-acre bog is flooded, the Haines & Haines crew harvests the crop, which will eventually go to Ocean Spray Cranberries Inc. for nationwide distribution.

Above: After the harvest, *"the prettiest scene in the temperate zone,"* cranberries are collected for transportation to processing plants.

New Jersey is America's third largest producer of cranberries, a fact attested to by this veritable sea of the scarlet fruit.

Overleaf: An autumn sunset burnishes the bog, denuded for another year.

At the Vandermark Glass House in Flemington's Liberty Village, the craft of glassblowing is kept alive by dedicated artisans.

GLASS & CHINA

Photographs by Klaus Schnitzer

THE AMERICAN COMIC WRITER, PETER De Vries, wrote of the conflicts between decoration and dining. "The food in museums," he complained in one novel, "is about on par with the murals in restaurants." Yet there are two neatly bipartisan products — porcelain and glass — which are comfortable and estimable in either place. They are sometimes art and other times utensils, objects and "objets," populating galleries as readily as galleys. The china of Lenox, which goes on special sale twice a year in one of the state's most rumbustious events, is also on display at the Smithsonian Institution. The fable and faunal figures of Cybis and Boehm inhabit the residences of plain working people as well as of countless royalty and men of state. Glass is equally commonplace — imagine the world without it, glass industry people like to say — and equally acclaimed, from collector's "Booz" bottles to sculpted vases. If photography, as described ironically by some, is "the art that everyone does," then glass, and to some extent porcelain, are "the arts that everyone acquires."

Though there is little connection between the two products, they do share many traits. They are both conceived from carefully prepared formulas — "slip" in the case of porcelain (a recipe that varies according to studio and is as fearfully guarded as a chef's fried chicken seasoning), and "batch" in the case of glass. Both require bracingly high degrees of heat, kilns supplying it for porcelain and furnaces for glass. Both are molded or sculpted according to design; and the designs often serve the same purposes — cups and saucers, plates and vases. Both are fragile, and are easily

converted to a heartbreaking splash of brilliant pieces by clumsy children or tempestuous spouses. And both are the products of great industries whose growth and history in the New World are inextricably tied to New Jersey.

A Palatinate German by the name of Casper Wistar, who was a "brass button worker" in Philadelphia, started the first glasshouse in New Jersey in 1739. Some attempts to manufacture glass in the American colonies had been tried before, the most notable being in Jamestown, Virginia, where, among other things, beads were made to becalm the Indians. This practice, the first industrial enterprise in the country, had no more success than the settlement. When Wistar began his glasshouse near Allowaystown, in Salem County, he knew little of glassmaking save that it was forbidden by the ruling British government. An unpropitious start for what he was to make a prosperous colonial industry.

Like any wise German who doesn't know exactly what to do, he sent for other Germans who did. Four arrived on a ship from Rotterdam to teach the art of glassmaking to Wistar and his son — and no one else. In exchange for the exclusive lessons, the craftsmen received land, food, servants, and materials for their factory. The site became known as Wistarberg and was in lively operation up until soon after the Revolutionary War, producing, as listed in an ad in the Pennsylvania Gazette, "Most sort of bottles . . . cafe bottles, snuff bottles, and mustard bottles, also electrifying globes and tubes, etc." What was not mentioned was that this enterprise also produced something of equal importance:

skilled workmen, the foundation of the nascent industry.

To look at a history of New Jersey glassmaking is almost like looking at a family tree, with Wistarberg as the roots and trunk. Out of this first glassworks emerged Jacob Stanger (spelling changed from Stenger), who came from a prodigious, productive, and all but ubiquitous family of German immigrants, at least one member of which seems, in the next 150 years, to have had a partnership in every other glassworks in the state. The Stangers' first site opened in 1775 in Glassboro; by the beginning of the nineteenth century they were represented, with the Union Glass Factory, near Millville, soon to be the "glass-making center of the state."

Millville is in the center of southern New Jersey, not far from the Delaware Bay. Its greatest attribute was, of course, sand — some of the best in the world, of a nearly pure silicon bioxide that gave a distinctive aquamarine green tint to the glass. Lime, which was also needed in the process (to give the glass stability), was obtained from ground-up oyster shells, fished from the bay. With the abundance of pine forests all around, fuel was no problem. And the proximity of navigable waterways leading to commercial centers like Philadelphia made the site all the more commendable.

Though there were glasshouses in other parts of the state, notably Jersey City, and one fledgling venture south of Belvidere, the majority of workers kept to the south. This they did with scant loyalty to any individual house. The men of the industry, from blowers to gatherers to gaffers (those who oversaw the shops), had dual reputations as hard workers and restless spirits. Most of them lived transient lives, based, one can't help but think, on the theory that "the glass is always greener on the other side. . . ." But it is owing to this chronic dissatisfaction that one can count, from the first Wistarberg to today, more than 200 known glass manufacturers in New Jersey — some of which, however, did not last more than a couple of years.

The men, especially the blowers, seem legendary now, with their headbands and charred gloves and trumpet-pouted cheeks, blowing at times more than 200 bottles a day, six days a week, in a velvety, Rembrandt-like glow. But it is by what they blew *after* those 200 bottles that we best remember them. For it was after the order had been filled that they could turn their attention to a wife's request or a boss's favor and let creativity and inspiration take over. And it was in these, the "end-of-the-day" items, that the South Jersey tradition was born.

In their book *American Glass,* George and Helen McKearin explain the style: "Since the blowers, whether in the late eighteenth or nineteenth century glasshouses, were under no compulsion to meet a current fashion in glassware, they formed their pieces as fancy or taste dictated. . . . But no matter how delicate or graceful in shape and decorative treatment, the pieces created by these blowers were invested with a quality of sturdiness rather than the feeling of fragility which characterizes more sophisticated wares. It is for these reasons that the glass in the South Jersey tradition has the intangible but distinctive characteristics of individuality and of the naiveté and peasant quality associated with folk art. In fact, it has often been called American folk art in glass."

The most common decoration of this style was the lily pad design, appearing with frequency on pitchers and bowls.

There were also more outlandish, or — as glass connoisseurs like to say — "historical" creations, such as the famous "Booz" bottle, a whiskey container in the form of a log cabin, created by the Whitney Glass Works. There were "whimsies" created, surely, on a whim, encompassing such items as powder horns, glass canes, witch balls, and spittoons. And, perhaps to mark the birth of a rampant bureaucracy, there was, in the late 1800s and early 1900s, the emergence of the paperweight. Ralph Barber, whose work in pitchers and vases is renowned, is still best known for the Millville rose, a paperweight he spent years perfecting before he went to Vineland to join one of New Jersey's few workers in art glass, Art Durand.

In the early twentieth century Michael Owens of Toledo, Ohio, invented the Owens Bottle Making Machine. Blasphemed by blowers, who ridiculed its abilities, it soon made them obsolete, along with their entire shops of gaffers, gatherers, cutters, and errand boys. It produced more glass less expensively than had ever been done before. An unqualified stroke of genius, it seemed; but, as any old timer will tell you, "you can't ask a machine to work overtime on a paperweight."

So romance gave way to economy, and an awesome industry grew. The peaceful, fiery, perfecting craft became a boisterous, flaming, mechanical operation. In the present-day Wheaton glass plant in Millville, four indomitable "Independent Section" machines surround every furnace. Each machine is a tall, skeletal structure, like an enormous mad organ gutted and drowned in ink-black grease. A glowing orange glob of liquid glass — a streak of portly lightning — flashes rashly into slots, where it is poured and pressed and lifted and molded by jerking, oozing flip-flop arms, amidst the odors of tar and smoke and the thunders of frenzied and unfettered machines, emerging finally on moving belts in the form of laboratory test tubes or canisters for Old Spice lotion.

In the Trenton studios of Cybis, in an almost monastic calm, clusters of women sit fastening arms onto toy-like figures. They are mounting the work of various artists — artists who, sequestered in a restricted chamber, design the sculptures. When assembled and puttied, the figure receives, from another cluster of women, any of several standard decorations. After perhaps several finishings, it enters the kiln. If it finishes the twenty-four hours of baking unscathed, it goes to be painted. Here, yet another cluster of women patiently dab it with colors, in a scene reminiscent of nothing so much as a Santa's workshop. Then come several more firings in the kiln, depending on the complexity. The changes here, it becomes obvious, have been less profound than those in the glass industry.

The porcelain industry grew up around Trenton in the mid nineteenth century for the same reasons that the glass industry grew up around Millville. The raw materials were there — in this case, clay deposits — the transportation lines were established, and the location was near commercial centers. Also, Trenton already had a prosperous pottery industry.

Two men by the names of Ott and Brewer, who ran Etruria Pottery in Trenton, introduced the manufacture of various sorts of both hard and soft paste porcelain to

America in 1863. They made many busts and figures of "Parian ware," a substance named after the marble of the Isle of Paros, which it was said to resemble. Their molder, Isaac Broome, was inspired, like many of his day, by the nation's centennial in 1876 and did busts of such disparate personages as Virgil, Ulysses S. Grant, and Cleopatra. These busts were said by many to be so good as to put him among the ranks of America's greatest sculptors. He is also the creator of the "Baseball Vase," a monument in porcelain to the national pastime, with three action figures — a winding-up pitcher, a cocked batter, and a fielding baseman — surrounding what, at first glance, looks like an ice cream cone but is actually a baseball set atop a sort of spiral.

Also from Etruria were William Bradley, who came from Ireland to produce the first Belleek ware in the United States, and a man by the name of Walter Scott Lenox. Lenox left Etruria and in the late 1880s founded what would eventually become the lodestar for American-made china. His company started out by making service plates, menu slabs, parasol handles, and inkstands; today Lenox furnishes tableware to the White House.

With such a reputation, it is understandable that Trenton was chosen by Boleslaw Cybis to be his new home. A Polish artist, he had come to New York to paint the murals at his country's pavilion in the 1939 World's Fair. His country was invaded that same year, in an act that commenced the Second World War, and he did not return. When he arrived in Trenton he found that it had suffered an opposite fate — desertion, at least by its pottery craftsmen. The renowned clay, too, was in short supply. But he stayed and, with his wife and a few artisans, began to make a reputation. The city also attracted Edward Marshall Boehm, a veterinarian and artist who was born in Baltimore and worked for a time in Long Island, and who, in Trenton, combined his two passions in porcelain. While many of Cybis's first efforts were on religious themes (the culmination of which was reached in the opulent "Child of Prague," now at the National Shrine of the Immaculate Conception in Washington, D.C.), Boehm's were of wild — and oftentimes barnyard — life: birds, horses, cows, dogs, and more birds. In addition to their acknowledged craftsmanship, both of these firms became adept at the equally delicate art of "official gift-giving" — from Cybis's Summit Conference Chess Set to Boehm's commemorative King Tut bust. Porcelain in hand, company representatives now spring up at world events with a perspicacious timing that causes political analysts and society hostesses alike to stammer in awe.

— *Thomas Swick*

One of the most exquisite and colorful sights in the industrial world today is the process of tempering hand-blown glass.

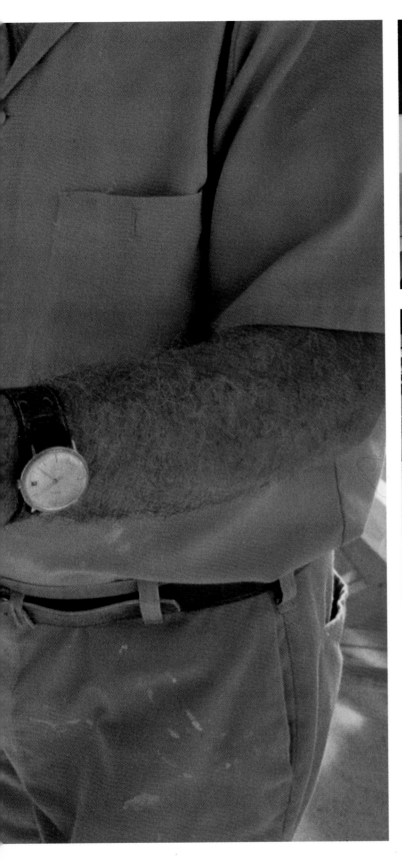

Left: The dexterous hands of an employee at Edward Marshall Boehm in Trenton extract a porcelain eagle's wing from its mold.

Top: The eagle, now fully assembled, is meticulously hand-painted in another step of its creation.

Above: Paying scrupulous attention to detail, an artisan at the General Mirror Corporation in Clifton adds finishing touches to her work.

Top: *Age-old techniques are adapted for the creation of this scientific vacuum vessel at the Mooney Brothers Corporation in Little Falls.*

Above: *The role of human hands and lungs is invaluable in the glassblowing process shown here at Scientific Glass – SGA, Inc. in Bloomfield.*

Opposite: *At Wheaton's Millville plant, this time exposure captures trails of molten glass on their way to be—coming beer bottles.*

Eyes riveted on her painstaking work, this woman lovingly shapes one of the china objects for which Lenox Inc. is renowned.

The sublime yet functional art of neon is displayed at Ryan Neon in Tenafly.

A veteran of many hours of firing and painting, this delicate porcelain figurine exemplifies the craftsmanship still practiced at Cybis studios in Trenton.

THE TOWN OF MORRISTOWN

MCMXVI

MUNICIPAL   BUILDING

The business of local government is conducted in the stately marble town hall of Morristown.

TOWN HALLS

Photographs by Langdon Clay

THERE IS NO LAW THAT SAYS EVERY municipality in New Jersey must own a building designated as town hall, city hall, or borough hall. But most places feel a need for such a structure, a need born of both practicality — meetings have to be held somewhere, and records stored — and a less tangible urge: a collective instinct reaching for identity, for accumulated common history.

Of the 567 municipalities in the state, those fifty to seventy-five that *don't* have town halls make for interesting cases. In Montague Township, population 2,000, perched on the northwestern tip of New Jersey, the town clerk, the engineer, and the tax assessor all keep their records in their own houses, and public meetings are held in the elementary school. (The nearest high school — and post office, for that matter — is in Port Jervis, New York.) There is something neighborly and reassuring about this arrangement: the government is not some abstraction; it is literally *of* the people. And yet there is something unsettling, too, about the absence of any enduring embodiment of the town, any permanent repository of its annals. The place outlives the people, and it ought to have its own home.

Common wisdom would suggest that town halls reflect the spirit and character of their towns. In some instances this is true. Sprawling Franklin Township, with 46.9 square miles, in 1972 built a sprawling, one-story town hall. In South Bound Brook, a charming little town of but one square mile and 5,000 residents, the nineteenth-century town hall is equally charming and equally modest. But such harmony is not universal. Affluent Princeton Township has as its town hall a rather plain yellow stucco house not far from a shopping center. And historic Princeton Boro, with its quiet colonial homes and neo-gothic university buildings, has a modern red brick hall, vintage 1967, that is surely attractive enough but that is, well, so very new. The City of Vineland, which is urban in nothing except its official status — Vineland is the center of South Jersey's rich farm country — chose to build an imposing office building that would look more at home in Dallas.

"Town halls are built to be functional, not beautiful or extravagant," says John Trafford, executive director of the New Jersey League of Municipalities. "Nobody has money to build Taj Mahals any more." Indeed, those communities that need new town halls are most likely to convert existing buildings. Schools, especially, tend to be recycled.

It is hard, anyway, to imagine local government, American style, going its mundane and sometimes rowdy way in a Taj Mahal. For most of the day, the town hall is the domain of functionaries, the stagehands and propmen of democracy. They see to it that all is ready for the weekly performances of such repertory companies as the zoning board, the planning board, the board of commissioners or committeemen or councilmen, and the ad hoc committee to study the traffic situation. Occasionally, of course, the zoning variance granted to the housing developer or the noxious odors from the landfill will bring out a large crowd bent on convincing the performers that, talented as they seem, they are but puppets of the people. Then the boundary between audience and actor vanishes, and in the fracas that follows, wisdom emerges, or sometimes chaos. Never mind. The town hall is built to accommodate such upheavals. It weathers and warps gracefully. However vicious the late-night meeting, the functionaries will return the next morning, and function. The town hall will settle down to business, and endure.

— *Paul Bradley*

The municipal building of Southampton Township, Vincentown, in Burlington County, dates back to 1884.

Vineland, in the center of South Jersey's rich farmland, has an imposing new city hall that would look more at home in Dallas.

The former Basking Ridge home of John Jacob Astor now serves as the town hall for Bernards Township.

Somerville, the county seat of Somerset, boasts a stately Gothic edifice for its municipal workings.

The machinations of democracy can take place anywhere, as evidenced here in Chatsworth by the mobile municipal hall of Woodland Township in Burlington County.

In Budd Lake, Mount Olive Township, a dance hall and casino from the thirties has been completely renovated and now houses government offices.

Few cities build ornate municipal halls anymore; Hoboken's reminds us of a time when they did.

In Morris County, Chester's borough hall was once a Roman Catholic church; much of the original interior architecture has been retained.

Another converted church building, this one in Great Meadows, Independence Township, gets a new lease on life as a town hall.

MALLS

Photographs by Joel Sternfeld

AH, TO SIT UNDER A SUN-ROOF WITH day's bounty bagged in prestigious logo at your side, nibbling on a morsel of Fiesta Burger or sucking out the last succulent chip from a famous chocolate cookie; sipping from your Coral Reef cup a non-carbonated nectar of Polynesian intent —and then to stir dreamily and ask of your loved ones, "Are you there?" and to hear in reply, from a kind stranger, "They beat out for the Space Port ages ago"; and so to linger more in paradise, enchanted by the parading forms, soothed by the gurgling fountains, lulled by the strains, falling like molecules upon the ear, as incorporeal as innocuous, of "Our Day Will Come."

Ah, yes, the Mall, whose very name becomes a sound of delectation and bulk: "Mmm — all!" The Mall, which has covered so many fields and converted so many faithful. Who among us has not been touched? Writing on the Mall in *The New Republic*, Neil Harris, a professor of history at the University of Chicago, stated that "the last architectural form that serviced the American dream so effectively were the movie palaces of the inter-war years." Not only do young people today flock to the Malls as their parents once did to the movie palaces — but so do their parents. The Mall has been charged with the slaying of the American downtown and called everything from a "buying machine" to "the modern equivalent of Coleridge's pleasure dome." "Xanadu in a parking lot," exclaimed *The Nation* in 1974. "The poor man's opera," declared George Sternlieb, Rutgers professor and mall chronicler. It has been likened to the Arab souk and hailed as the successor to the Village Green. Writing

without a trace of historical condescension, Victor Gruen, the developer of the nation's first large enclosed mall (Southgate Shopping Center in Minneapolis), pronounced that the Mall "can provide the need, place, and opportunity for participation in modern community life that the ancient Greek Agora, the Medieval Market Place, and our own Town Squares provided in the past." It is also, less manifestly, a wayward kin to the great cathedrals of Europe.

Whether it ". . . squats on the urban and suburban landscape . . ." (Jennifer Cross, *The Nation*), or ". . . floats on the landscape like a pyramid . . ." (Joan Didion, *Esquire*), or whether, "seen from the outside, from its vast acreage of parking lots . . . [it] looks like a pile of blocks" (Neil Harris, *The New Republic*), it is to many Americans a source of inspiration. (It has, however, hardly entered our songs, our paintings, our movies, our arts — though most of them have entered it.)

It dominates and serves the suburb just as the cathedral did the town. It is peopled by its own parishioners and occasioned by pilgrims, trekking mostly for the great feast days (Thanksgiving weekend, pre-Christmas, White Sales, Summer Clearance) and the personal celebrations (Graduation, Mother's and Father's Days). There are the devout, who attend most every day, and the once-a-week believers.

But it is in the basic design that one sees the unmistakable similarity. As in the great cathedrals, there is a chief place of congregation (a major department store), one or two lesser points (the large discount stores), and a passage connecting numerous small specialized, boutique-like side chambers for more personal oblations. This is the great concourse where you stroll curiously, meeting fellow pilgrims and eyeing agreeably the suburbanites as they sit or wander, interspersing consumer litanies with local gossip. And as you walk, you peer into the alluring shops, each with its own peculiar incense and icons. There is a continuous flow, from morning to night, when at last the great doors close and you enter out into the world again, if not richer in spirit, at least poorer in purse, and with a similar sense of well-being. Something within you has been fulfilled.

In the beginning was the Garden State Plaza, a group of shops that opened in Paramus in 1957, becoming New Jersey's first authentic shopping center — albeit uncovered. (These hatless malls are seldom built today and so venture to become National Historic Landmarks in the near, destructive future.) The state's first enclosed mall (for the fastidious historians among us) was the Cherry Hill Mall, one hundred shops put under one roof by The Rouse Company of Maryland. It had a phenomenal success. Bus tours were run to it as if to, well, a cathedral, and few left unimpressed. There are those who can still remember their mothers returning from a bridge club excursion and telling at the evening dinner, in awed, almost reverential tones, of their "day at the Cherry Hill Mall." James W. Rouse was to become to New Jersey malls what O. H. Ammann had been to New Jersey bridges. From this early success he went on to create the Echelon Mall, the Paramus Park, and the grandest in the state, the Willowbrook and Woodbridge Malls. New Jersey, with its dense, suburban populations, was found to be fecund territory. In Paramus, malls pullulated until there were five separate ones within five square miles: a mall empyrean unequaled virtually anywhere. By 1978 more than twenty-six malls were up and operating, and the chimes of their registers rang out over New Jersey the highest gross income per square foot of any malls in the country.

Like cathedrals, all malls are similar, though no two are ever the same. There is always the vast desert of macadam surrounding the unfathomed, but not unlettered, walls (upon which scrolls of Goliath proportion hang like nonflying buttresses). Inside there is the ineluctable vista of fountain, tree, and "impulse shopper" highlighted in a pastiche of ceramic tile and park-like benches. There are in every mall, it seems, the mallwalk cafes, the cookie outlets with their salesgirls in colonial petticoats, the cheese shops (red barn facade) with their salesgirls in equally stunning Alpine garb, the unavoidable shoe stores, the most intriguingly named "Vision Centers," the coyly named "Jekyll's Hide," "Card-O-Rama," "Wild Pair," "Jeans West," "Good Grief," "Pet Pourri" . . . the Earring Gazebos, the Radio Shacks and Record Museums, the de-mustyfied Waldenbooks and Dalton Books, the Limiteds and the Gaps, the

144

very sporting Herman and the very gifty Spencer.

Yet New Jersey can rightly boast a wondrous variety of malls — malls that loom like bunkers out of woodland and malls that wait openly for unwary souls at highway exits. There are malls of every class, from the "nouveau richesse" of Riverside Square to the proletarian Menlo Park. Paramus Park possesses one of the finest two-story calibrated waterfalls in malldom, while Riverside Square has parquet floors on its second level and stairways and highlights of genuine oak. The mall at Short Hills is largely sartorial, while Paramus Park is wildly gustatorial. There are no-nonsense malls such as the Fashion Center, and "hang-out" malls like Quaker Bridge and Willowbrook. It is to these latter malls, with their movie theaters and Space Ports (those electronic-game-and-pinball rooms), that sociologists come to study and pedestrians to gaze. And what sights to be seen! The old men sitting by the fountains, improbably hatted in the controlled environment. Space Port "technicians" in blue jump suits bearing mock NASA patches, changing quarters for kids; and the kids, absorbed, standing in the preferred posi-

tion (palms flat on either side of the machine, right leg crossed at the ankle over left), their faces lit by a febrile rose glow. Young parents and oft-times grandparents pushing their babies in carriages that look like upside down Ys on wheels. A rotund, sun-tanned woman in a tent dress holding by the handles a sack that reads: "Big Brown Bag." Somewhere in a department store a tired, frowzy old woman sitting with her head in her hands between two frolicsome, nattily impervious young mannequins. (So many mannequins, to live on stylishly while we die out of fashion!) The slender salesgirl who inherits, by the magic of mirrors, the fatty calves of her counter client. The sunglasses that must be tried with the sales-tag dancing about the nose, like a small kite, and the horrendous heresy of comment — "They look great!" — to close out the deal. The dull human head poking discreditably out of a menagerie of furry pandas and cuddly bears. And all the people walking with one phrase on their lips, the very phrase for which the malls, in all their majesty, were built: "Just looking."   — *Thomas Swick*

PATERSON

Photographs by Michael Spozarsky

THE PLACE TO BEGIN A TOUR OF Paterson's Historic District is where the city itself began — at the falls. You can stand suspended on a bridge built at a height equal to the drop — 77 feet — and gaze, as men of vision, both prosaic and poetic, have gazed in the past. Well before there was a bridge, or even a town, Alexander Hamilton picnicked on these cliffs and conceived the idea of an industrial city, constructed and sustained on the natural power generated by the Great Falls of the Passaic. Hamilton was then urging America to change from an agrarian to an industrial society, warning that, were the change not made, she would be forever dependent on England. In 1791 he encouraged the founding of the Society of Useful Manufactures (SUM), and Paterson, named after then Governor William Paterson, became the first planned industrial city in the country. Nearly two centuries later, a Paterson doctor and poet, William Carlos Williams, came just as intuitively to the falls and interpreted them as a literary force, hearing in their constant, unintelligible roar a voice, of a city and a people, wanting to communicate itself. From Book I of his four-volume poem *Paterson*:

> *the river comes pouring in above the city*
> *and crashes from the edge of the gorge*
> *in a recoil of spray and rainbow mists—*
>
> *(What common language to unravel?*
> *. . . combed into straight lines*
> *from that rafter of a rock's*
> *lip.)*

Still standing on that edge of the bridge, usually safe from spray, you can peer down into the marble-churned, bouldered basin and marvel at those who've mocked its majesty, jumped, and survived. The most notable of these leapers was Sam Patch — "The Great Descender, Mighty Patch!" — who jumped in to retrieve a rolling pin that fell out during ceremonies to open the bridge. Thus began a career of country-wide leaps and bounds that ended, after a slip at the Genesee Falls, with Sam frozen in a floating block of ice in Lake Ontario. If you look up across the low bridge of Wayne Avenue, just above the falls, you can see the spot where John P. Holland tested the first successful submarine. (A picture in the Paterson Museum shows a pesky, bespectacled Irishman in a bowler hat popping up from the lid of his homemade creation, whose sole reason of invention, he claimed, was "to blow up the bloody British navy!") Bringing your eyes back across the falls you see to your right a couple of small brick gate houses and the Great Falls Park, formerly a municipal dump. Then you turn your back to the falls and imagine a wire, ascending from the low south bank to the rocky precipice at the north, traversed by Philippe Petit and the late Karl Wallenda, men whose chosen aerialist sites are testament to a commanding, authentic grandeur. (Now young men can sometimes be seen winning bets by standing at the cliff's soggy edge for the count of ten.) Looking across the river, your back still to the falls, you gaze upon the buildings of the historic district; the saw-tooth-roof mills shouldering the river and the giraffe-neck smokestacks punctuating the sky. And looking upon this scene, you need no imagination. For it is, physically, as it was.

Once across the river and looking down Spruce Street, you will find a mill town scene of astounding harmony. The thoroughfare, neither wide nor narrow, is bordered on either side by solid, red-brick, high-windowed factories that frame the grassy dome of Garret Mountain, at whose base the street's proud progress absurdly ends. All is concise and compact — factory, factory, factory, mountain. The sidewalks are skinny, barren, treeless — mandating a neighborhood of toilers. The only shade, apart from the factories' own grave evening shadows, is in the form of worthless, random strips from telephone wires dangled and crisscrossed overhead. You sense that, were you to wait a few hours, you would hear the work whistles blow and see the streets fill with hundreds of foundrymen and shopgirls, heading home.

The factory on the right still bears the lettering: "Paterson Silk Machinery Exchange — Looms — Warpers — Winders — Quillers — Coppers — Jacquards." By the mid nineteenth century the silk industry had begun in Paterson, and toward the end of that century the city was combatively called "The Lyons of the New World." The silk mills alone numbered over 300, employing more than 18,000 workers, not to mention those in related industries — silk braiding, weaving, and dyeing; jute, flax, and hemp; tools, gears, and castings. It is said that, even before this surge, George Washington, at his inaugural, "wore a coat of crow-black homespun woven in Paterson." The Jacquard loom, "the Cadillac of textile machinery," was devised and first set to work in the city's mills.

> Machines in haughty and presumptuous pride
> Are mankind magnified.

>> ——FROM "ODE TO MACHINES," BY LOUIS GINSBERG,
>> PATERSON POET AND SCHOOLTEACHER, LATE
>> FATHER OF POET ALLEN GINSBERG.

The large, second building on the left as you look down Spruce Street is the Rogers Locomotive Erecting Shop, built in 1871. About the same time that the silk industry was beginning, Thomas Rogers withdrew from textile manufacturing and ventured into the locomotive industry. A steam engine had come over from England, and, showing enterprising faculty, he dismantled it, studied it, and put it back together again. Soon he was putting together his own. At the height of his production a locomotive was rolling out of his factory every two days, pulled by horses to the rails across town. Within fifty years, five other locomotive firms were established in Paterson, producing a good many of the engines that settled the West. In 1836 Samuel Colt, of the notable Paterson cotton manufacturing family, invented the Colt revolver and soon afterward began turning them out in great numbers. Now there were both engines to move the pioneers and guns to arm them. If, as it is said, "The Battle of Waterloo was won on the playing fields of Eton," then, without a doubt, the American West was won in the factory houses of Paterson. It was here, years later at the Wright Aeronautical Corporation, that the engine for Charles Lindbergh's "Spirit of St. Louis" was manufactured. As Christopher Norwood has written in her book *About Paterson*: "Paterson did not only manufacture; it produced articles that redefined the limits of life. It is impossible to think of any other city whose products cut so deeply into the texture of the United States and not only transformed its national character, but revolutionized American relations with the world."

The city swelled with immigrants — English, Irish, Italians, Germans, Jews, Dutch, Poles. Its population increased 50 percent every decade, so that until 1900 it was the fastest growing city on the East Coast.

In 1913, Paterson suffered a strike from which some say it has never fully recovered. Twenty-five thousand silk workers refused to man the mills and were supported in their abstention by the International Workers of the World. Now the names of Big Bill Haywood and Elizabeth Gurley Flynn (the leaders of the IWW) are spoken in Paterson with the same reverence once reserved for Rogers and Colt. But however heroic, the strike began the eclipse of a heyday. Soon the emergence of a new technology and the accessibility of fresher sites closed many of the factories and silenced much of the city, until the roar of the falls once again held sway.

In 1968, a group of Columbia University students in restoration architecture came to Paterson. They examined the buildings and made drawings showing their aesthetic potential if restored. Mary Ellen Kramer, the wife of the mayor, Lawrence "Pat" Kramer, was intrigued by the results. The problem, however, was that a contract had already been signed for a highway, Route 20, to cut through the center of that very district. But they were not discouraged, and they did not leave. John Young, a member of the student Urban Deadline group, stayed four years, lending a dedicated, invaluable service to the salvage effort. With Mary Ellen Kramer they formed the Great Falls Development Corporation and called for "a modest change in the road." Says Kramer, "We never said 'no road.' We would have gotten our heads kicked in. It was a time when the philosophy was 'highways save cities.' We had to demonstrate that there was a value in the district." As it happened, confrontation with the road never presented itself. The first important action came in 1971, when the district was put on the National Register of Historic Places. Soon afterward, national experts arrived from institutions such as New Jersey Historical Sites, National Trust, and Smithsonian. "It was very important," says Kramer, "for people from the outside to come and to say what we knew but what Paterson had not thought about." The city began to react. "People saw the city differently," she adds. "Public officials had reason to take another look." The dump near the falls was made into a park, with lights, a bridge, walkways, and walls donated by various private and civic concerns. At its opening a ceremony was held that became the first of the annual Great Falls Festivals.

Then came a disheartening battle to lose, one that seemed to prick the very fragile fabric of the cause. Passaic County Community College was looking for a campus, and a proposal had been made to center it in the district, with several abandoned mills serving as college halls. The plan's ultimate rejection pointed, bleakly, to a certain undesirability of the real estate. "There are problems with mills," admits Kramer. "They are grimy. They are industrial. George Washington did not sleep there." They are, someone else has confided, "not a DAR number."

> old clerks in their asylums of fat, the slobs and
> dumbbells of the ego with money and power . . .

> harridan vision of electricity at night and
> daylight misery of thumb-sucking rage.

>> ——FROM "PATERSON," BY ALLEN GINSBERG.

But the struggle to salvage the district went on. In 1976 this first planned American industrial city experienced another first. In ceremonies officiated by President Gerald

Ford, the district — forty-nine buildings and 119 acres — became the first industrial area in the United States to be designated a National Historic Landmark.

The Union Works Mill is one of its first success stories. It is an inspiring story to tell, and an inspiring story to hear — of a building in which children once labored for pennies an hour, transformed into a school in which they now learn to read and write. The non-graded elementary school is called "Dawn Treader" and was started by the Evangelical Committee for Urban Ministries in Paterson. It occupies the second floor of the mill, in a bright, flowing, unpartitioned area, while above it a craft workshop is housed. The mill, which ceased operation in 1937, had sat for decades, like many of its neighbors, abandoned and abused. Now its brick is swept with uncommon spruceness and its windows are festooned with the cut-outs of schoolchildren.

Yet the Rogers Shop next door is the district's gem. There must be a dozen Patersonians alone who call it, with artful obeisance, "my baby." Working with an Economic Development Administration grant, the city built itself a castle from grime. The task was herculean. First — a requisite for funding from the federal government — archaeologists made diggings on the site. Known as "industrial archaeologists," they search an area for tools or machines or handworks, the buried flotsam and jetsam of a lost industrial period. Because records were seldom kept of industrial processes, the archaeologists' finds often give clues about how certain systems or technologies, now obsolete, developed and grew. One such lost technology in Paterson involves the factories' use of raceways — or canals — as power for their foundries. In Paterson's historic district, forge drop hammers, pits filled with iron scalings, and 300 metal files were uncovered, along with numerous bottles, combs, doll limbs, smoking pipes, and checker chips.

With the Rogers Shop itself, not a shortcut was taken. The seeming infinity of brick was not sandblasted, but flushed with water. The mortar for new wall sections was tested and set to correspond to the pattern of the old, so that only a discerning eye can see at first glance the difference between the two when they connect. The large wooden portals that line Spruce Street, grand enough to push a locomotive through, are reproductions of the original ones. Wherever possible, authentic hardware was used — on the side doors and trusses it can be seen, scrubbed of paint, and picturesque. The windows were all replaced; now they are double-hung behind double-hung, the pride of Gordon Ash, a consultant who is managing construction of the historic district buildings. "They aren't like in the dinosaur buildings you find today, where you can't get any air. One window in each bay opens out, just like they used to," he says, standing on the polished fourth floor of the building. "When it's warm you just open them up," and he performs the task in ready delight. "Back to normalcy," he says.

But the Rogers Shop is not only a model for building restoration — "This building was done with care, integrity, and love," says Ash. "We've set the criteria for what others should approach" — it is a model as well for building use. Apart from a downstairs museum (old Engine 299, recently acquired from Panama, stands outside), there are office spaces (the second floor is occupied by the U.S. Census Bureau) and facilities for seminars, conferences, and recep-

tions. It is an example of what Community Development people in Paterson call, in extraordinary doses, "adaptive reuse."

Paterson is a town that talks in prefixes, especially the prefix "re." It is difficult to speak to anyone, especially one concerned with the district, without hearing mention of reuse, rebirth, refurbishment; rejuvenation, revitalization, rehabilitation; renovation, restoration, renaissance. But reuse (adaptive) is their beloved.

The district represents different things to different people. Sid Willis, director of the Department of Community Development, sees Paterson as "a gritty city wanting to capitalize on its industrial past...doing something with what we have, rather than going off in some false direction." Constance Ramirez, an historical and archaeological consultant to the project, calls it "preservation in the sense of protecting and interpreting...taking remnants, like the ruins in the Roman Forum, and working with what is authentic." It is unanimously agreed that the district should not become a museum, set off in time — Mayor Kramer cautions mercilessly against what he calls "purple ropes and old ladies in cotton dresses" — but an arena growing and changing in time. Some see this in terms of an urban industrial park. Others, pointing to the impracticality of heavy industry in such a dense area (Paterson itself has approximately 140,000 people in only eight square miles), see an outgrowth of offices and white collar jobs. A few mills are designated to become artists' lofts, and everyone, it seems, looks to artists as a key component. "Artists," they say, "bring in a tremendous life force." And they mention SoHo in Manhattan. Walking past a forlorn mill, they talk of artists' studios and galleries, boutiques and specialty shops, cafes and restaurants. They refer boldly to Ghirardelli Square in San Francisco and Faneuil Hall in Boston and hope that, as in those places, the spirit, once started, will spread to other sections of the city.

The Historic District of Paterson is conveniently near to New York, in an already heavily populated area of New Jersey. It is just off major highways and easily found by relatively directionless and disoriented motorists. Its falls, the second largest in the Northeast, are becoming known even to unversed Jerseyans. Yet the district suffers one problem that sets it apart from the previously mentioned models. Boston and San Francisco each were able to work with the amenities and frills of former times. Paterson was not.

Paterson, and especially its Mill District, was a grisly place. The people who lived and worked there — men, women, and children — mostly worked. The growing wealth of the mill owners was rarely spent on the city, but rather on opulent estates, such as Lambert Castle, well outside the town. The citizens of the city, the workers, had little time for leisure and even fewer places in which to take it. A proposal to build sidewalks for their streets was passed only after bitter and unsanctimonious debate. The workers were regarded merely as tools in the process of production, and their welfare was not a conceivable concern. As Christopher Norwood explained in her book: "Paterson was not designed as a city; it was designed as a corporation." Which makes its phoenix-like resurrection in the twentieth century more arduous, yet all the more remarkable.

— *Thomas Swick*

The North Jersey Philharmonic rehearses in the musicians' local union hall on Prospect Street.

In a previous life, the union hall housed the horse-drawn trucks of Paterson's fire department.

LOCAL 248 AMERICAN FEDERATION OF MUSICIANS

The restored facade of Local 248 stands as a glowing example of Paterson's commitment to its past.

A Rogers locomotive, Engine 299 was shipped to Panama for use in canal building, and was returned to Paterson in 1979.

"Paterson did not only manufacture; it produced articles that redefined the limits of life" — another view of the Rogers Shop.

The fourth floor of the restored Rogers Locomotive Erecting Shop provides facilities for seminars, conferences, and art shows.

The Rogers Shop is a model for industrial building restoration and reuse. Its new double thermopane windows allow for an efficient flow of air on hot days.

Many locomotives passed through these massive wooden doors of the Rogers Shop on Spruce Street, which have been faithfully restored to their former grandeur down to the authentic hardware.

In the nineteenth century, an abundance of factories like the Paterson Silk Machinery Exchange earned the city its nickname "The Lyons of the New World."

This serene-looking body of water is the middle raceway of a three-tiered system that powered the Phoenix Silk Mill on Van Houten Street during Paterson's industrial heyday.

Tony Morello is one of the artists who have renovated lofts on downtown Main Street, contributing to the city's cultural renaissance.

A sweeping vista of Paterson includes Garret Mountain and Great Falls Park, site of an annual Labor Day festival.

The sun sets on Garret Mountain, a snowy dome at whose base lies the country's first planned industrial city.

High Point State Park

Nicholas Foster

Victorian Cape May

Jeremiah Bean

Nassau Hall

Dan Katz

The State House, Trenton

Island Beach State Park

EPILOGUE

THE PRECEDING CHAPTERS HAVE explored much of what is little-known or unexpected in New Jersey in an effort to paint a kaleidoscopic picture of the state's diversity. As such, this is an incomplete portrait, telling much but certainly not all of our story. In closing, therefore, it seems appropriate to pay tribute to some of the more obvious, well-known facets of the state's landscape, both literally and figuratively.

In a literal sense, landscape is what New Jersey is all about. From High Point in the Northwest corner, where the Appalachian Trail crosses into the state, to the delicate filigrees of Cape May Victorian houses facing the sea some two hours south, New Jersey offers a variety of visual and physical pleasures and opportunities unrivaled anywhere. Dotting the landscape in between these two points are more figurative elements, historic places calling to mind the seminal importance the state has played in the history of the United States. In the center of the state, for instance, lies Princeton's Nassau Hall, built as a place of study but used by the first Congress as the formal seat of government for the new nation in the formative years of the Republic. Likewise, the battlefields near Jockey Hollow in Morristown, where Washington's beleaguered army spent a winter as bad as that at Valley Forge, recall how the peculiar geographic location of the state has influenced its role in history. Situated between the two colonial capitals of New York and Philadelphia, New Jersey today is the home for millions who live side by side with these monuments and many more like them. These are New Jersey's more obvious, "expected" pleasures, and in a brief, closing tribute to so many like them which our limits of both time and space forced us to avoid, we offer here a variety of friendly and familiar perspectives.

163

CREDITS

Designer, Creative Director ....Lawrence Barth
Editor ....Daniel Laskin
Copy Editor, Captions ....Janet Bukovinsky
Production Consultant....................Caldecot Chubb
Production Assistants ....Leslie Flis
                                      Kenneth Newbaker
Research...............................Phillip Longman

Thomas Swick grew up in Phillipsburg, New Jersey and worked as a feature writer for the *Trenton Times*. More recently he has traveled and freelanced, writing a collection of travel stories and teaching English in Poland and Greece.

Lynn Asinof, a former Chicago newspaper reporter, is a freelance writer who specializes in transportation and regional planning. Her articles have appeared in *New Jersey Monthly*, the *Chicago Sun-Times*, *Detroit News*, and *Business Week*.

Paul Bradley is a freelance writer based in New Jersey. A former correspondent for the *New York Times*, his work has also appeared in *New Jersey Monthly*, *Philadelphia Magazine*, and *Connecticut Magazine*.

Phillip Longman is a writer-researcher at *New Jersey Monthly*.

Daniel Laskin (editor) has been the managing editor of *New Jersey Monthly*, a staff writer for *Horizon*, and a newspaper reporter in both New Jersey and Vermont. His writing has appeared in *Esquire*, the *New York Times*, and the *Washington Post*.

We would also like to thank the following people, whose help on this book has been invaluable:

Patricia Gaby
Alan Glass
William J. Healy
Eileen Lawton
Leo M. Murray
Jerry Nussbaum
Richard F. Ober Jr.
MaryAnn Pezzullo
Norman Sanders
Lenore Smith
Joseph Timko
Richard C. Woodbridge
General Dynamics Corp.
Paterson Department of Community Development
Passaic County Historical Society
Trenton Public Library
Pennsylvania State Museum
New Jersey State Museum
Joseph Falcohn
Campbell Soup Co.
New Jersey Historical Society
Hoffman-La Roche
Rutgers University Library
General Foods
The Port Authority of NY and NJ
New Jersey Turnpike Authority
R.C.A. Laboratories
Edison National Historic Site
Paterson Museum
The Board of Directors of United Jersey Banks